Native American Mythology in Modern American Literature

Native American Mythology in Modern American Literature:

Analysis of the Novels
House Made of Dawn by N. Scott Momaday
and *Ceremony* by Leslie Marmon Silko

Oksana Danchevskaya

Cover: *Made of Dawn* by Oksana Danchevskaya
Copyright © 2017 Oksana Danchevskaya

CreateSpace, Charleston SC
Copyright © 2017 Oksana Danchevskaya
All rights reserved.
ISBN: 1548511013
ISBN-13: 978-1548511012

In memory of Alexander Vaschenko,
a wonderful Mentor,
a brilliant scholar, a gifted teacher,
a true friend and a unique
great-hearted person

CONTENTS

Introduction   8
Chapter 1. Native American Mythology   12
  1.1. "Myth", "Holy Story", "Legend" and Other Important Notions   12
  1.2. Myth and Ritual. Storytelling   20
  1.3. An Overview of Native American Mythology   26
Chapter 2. Native American Writers   48
Chapter 3. An Overview of American Indian History   53
Chapter 4. The Analysis of *House Made of Dawn* and *Ceremony*   64
  4.1. N. Scott Momaday and Leslie Marmon Silko   64
  4.2. The Use of American Indian Mythology in the Novels   73
  4.3. *House Made of Dawn*   77
  4.4. *Ceremony*   88
  4.5. Comparison of *House Made of Dawn* and *Ceremony*   104
  4.6. The Role of Stories, Songs and the Word for American Indians   106
Conclusion   113
Bibliography   118

INTRODUCTION

> *The mythology and ritual are the heart, the lifeblood, of every Native American culture.*
>
> S.D. Gill, I.F. Sullivan, *Dictionary of Native American Mythology*

American literature is rich in books of all genres and authors of all races. Still, there is a special category of writers who started to appear only about a century ago, but have claimed a very important place in the world literature – Native Americans. They are a special phenomenon as they are unusual among other representatives of this kind of art. In spite of a relatively recent appearance of American Indian literature for the general reader, many Native American tunes were already used long ago by white writers – probably, Henry Longfellow's *The Song of Hiawatha* may serve the brightest example, based completely on the legends, beliefs and history of a concrete tribe – the Odjibwe, and some others.

Everything connected with ancient culture is very interesting and involving, and especially if it is possible to look at it from various angles (as many American Indian authors do). That is why our book is not restricted to literature and the stylistic usage of mythology in it. Only through some knowledge of history, traditions and beliefs of a people one can understand its literature, and Native American one is full of symbols, allegories and traditional stories. For an unprepared reader it is not always easy to grasp the whole, or sometimes even hidden, meaning of a novel, a story, or a poem, but having some background knowledge will help here.

The major goal of this book is to analyze the use of Native American mythology in the two selected novels by American Indian writers and to try to comprehend what is meant by "the word" for Native Americans. There are also several minor objectives:

1) to give an idea about myth and mythology in general and Native American mythology in particular with a special accent of Pueblo mythology (as the protagonists of the books are Pueblos);

2) to analyze the role of mythology, storytelling and songs in Native American culture;

3) to give a short account of Native American literature and authors;

4) to give an overview of the history of American Indians on the territory of what is now the United States;

5) to analyze the use of American Indian myths in the two novels, their purpose and effects;

6) to analyze the attitude to and the "relationship" with the word among American Indians and to compare them to those among the whites.

Nevertheless, we understand that it is hardly possible to give a full coverage of all the above-mentioned subtopics; thus, ours is just an attempt to present a general overview of some of the most important aspects of Native American culture related to literature and to offer our interpretation of the novels.

The two books chosen for this purpose are *House Made of Dawn* by N. Scott Momaday and *Ceremony* by Leslie Marmon Silko. There are numerous reasons for such a combination of works, here we will indicate only several: similar ideas and messages, similar lives of the protagonists (a Pueblo Indian Abel and a half-breed Pueblo Indian Tayo), similar background of the novels, almost the same time when they were written (*House Made of Dawn* – 1968, *Ceremony* – 1977), and finally similar origins of the authors. At the same time, both novels are very interesting from the stylistic point of view and because of their composition; besides, they are one of the best samples of Native American writing.

Chapter 1. Native American Mythology
1.1. "Myth", "Holy Story", "Legend" and Other Important Notions

First of all, it is necessary to work on the notions "myth", "mythology", "legend", "holy story" and the like. It is not an easy task as those terms can often be used interchangeably; besides, the approaches to their classification differ. Here we will try to mention only a few — the most relevant, in our opinion — definitions.

In most cases, folklore texts can be clearly divided into myths, historical traditions and legends, but sometimes it is not so easy to draw a clear line between them. There are some parameters [...]: 'the myth is fabulous and sacred; the historical tradition is not fabulous and nonsacral'[1]. 'Legends are associated mainly with the characters of sacred history, while historical traditions — with the characters of worldly history, and the element of miraculous is not necessary in them'; 'The legend in comparison with the myth is less sacral and it describes later events than the ones in the myth', it 'takes place between the myth and the historical

---

[1] Токарев, С.А. (ред.). Мифы народов мира: Энциклопедия в 2 т. М.: Советская Энциклопедия, 1991. Т.1. С. 572.

description'[2], but 'the action of the historical traditions occurs only in the historical time'[3].[4]

According to *Webster Dictionary*, "myth" is "a usually traditional story of ostensibly historical events that serves to unfold part of the world view of a people or explain a practice, belief, or natural phenomenon"; "mythology" is "a body of myths: as *a*: the myths dealing with the gods, demigods, and legendary heroes of a particular people"[5], while "legend" is "a story coming down from the past; *especially*: one popularly regarded as historical although not verifiable."[6] To enlarge the definition of myth, which in the most general sense refers to any invented story, we will refer to it in our research as to a "traditional story, usually very old, which has or once had significant spiritual, moral, or social significance."[7] For a better understanding it is important to describe what myth is not.

---

[2] Ibid., T.2. C. 45.
[3] Ibid., c. 333.
[4] Данчевская, О.Е. Исторические предания, легенды и мифы севеоамериканских индейцев как дополнительный этнологический источник // Источники и историография по антропологии народов Америки. М.: ИЭА РАН, 2017. С. 261-274. С. 272.
[5] Webster Dictionary, [online] Available at: <http://www.webster.com> [Accessed 25 March 2002].
[6] Ibid.
[7] alt.mythology General FAQ ver. 1.8, [online] Available at: <http://members.bellatlantic.net/~vze33gpz/mythgenfaq.html#A2A> [Accessed 05 April 2002].

Stories which, from their origin, are set in print and passed down unchanged are not myth. Myth is a form of folklore, which means that it is shaped by the "folk" in general, and not just one or a few authors. Many myths are collected in books, but they have had long oral traditions before that. Second, folklore is not myth if it is not a story, so proverbs, superstitions, riddles, etc. are not myths as such.[8]

Most stories associated with current religions are, by definition, myths. Professionals distinguish between mythology, legend, and folklore.

Very briefly, myths are considered true by the people who tell them; they are usually set near the beginning of time and often concern the origins of things. Legends are also regarded as true, but are set later in history when the world was much as it is today. Folklore is considered false by the people telling it, and its setting in time and space is usually irrelevant. Myths are considered sacred, legends are more often secular, and folktales aren't taken seriously (although the overall message might be).[9]

---

[8] Ibid.
[9] Ibid.

In this book we will use the words "myth" and "story" (normally meaning a "holy story") interchangeably understanding under them any description, in prose or in poetry, of events that are historical or regarded as such by American Indians and are part of Native American mythology. In the understanding of American Indian myths and mythology we agree with the authors of *Dictionary of Native American Mythology* and take the same position as theirs. They believe that mythology is a term that has received much attention by academic communities. Many have wanted to separate myth from tale, legend, and other forms of story. Some argue that myth refers primarily to "religious" stories that tell or describe the creation and origin of the world. We have not made any such distinction. We have considered as myth any story that reflects the quality and character of a specific Native American culture, or of Native American cultures more generally.[10] To narrow the definition of a story, we will also use such notions as "song", which for us is a story presented in a poetical form and performed in singing, and "chant", which is any song used for

---

[10] Austgen, S.M. Leslie Marmon Silko's Ceremony and the Effect of White Contact on Pueblo Myth and Ritual, [online] Available at: <http://history.hanover.edu/hhr/hhr93_2.html> [Accessed 14 January 2007]. P. XI.

sacred purposes, such as healing, ritual praying or accompanying any ceremonies. Many American Indian songs can be identified as prayers because of their contents and aim. Thus, in Native American mythology among myths, holy stories, legends, historical traditions, etc. we find songs and chants, stories in prose and stories in poetry. They all combined give a full idea of the forms in which American Indian mythology is presented. If we are to study myth closer, it becomes obvious that it also deals with religion and philosophy.

This is also the history of "pre-history", an attempt to tell us what could happen before the written history of mankind began. This is also the oldest form of literature, which usually existed in the form of folklore. Myth told the ancient people who they were and how to live. Thus, myth used to be and still remains the basis of moral, state and national self-conscience.[11]

Myth cannot be referred only to "primitive" conscience – even nowadays life is full of mythological symbols and meanings, of mythological language, and we all still preserve the archetypal consciousness to some extent. All this is a very important part of human heritage. Fables, fairy tales, literature, epos, sacred books

---

[11] Бирлайн, Дж.Ф. Параллельная мифология. Москва: КРОН-ПРЕСС, 1997. С. 14.

of various religions – they all include ancient myths that have gone beyond time, distance or cross-cultural differences. A very interesting fact is that myths in their pure form are very similar with different peoples, even for those who live far from each other.[12] Probably that is one of the factors why they still exist and are treated with so much attention by both the peoples who preserve them and by the scientists who study them. And that is why they continue to live and function in contemporary fiction (in our case – in American Indian fiction) with unfading success.

Mythology is common to the whole mankind, but it is presented in different forms. What forms of mythological literatures are there? First of all, this is *myth* itself. Then there is *legend*, which is very close to fable – "a legendary story of supernatural happenings". There are also *sagas*, but they mainly deal with Icelandic and Norwegian myths. Taking the moral function into consideration, there is *parable* – "a usually short fictious story that illustrates a moral attitude or a religious principle", *allegory* – "a literary form that tells a story to present a truth or enforce a

---

[12] There is even a special academic field which studies such parallel motifs — Comparative Mythology. One of the most prominent contemporary researchers in this area is Yuri Beryozkin who has been studying in detail the areal distribution of folklore motifs.

moral", and *apologue* – "an allegorical narrative usually intended to convey moral."[13] We can see that these forms are interrelated and sometimes may even stand one for another. As to the notions defining a people's cultural background, there is *mythology*[14], *tradition* – "1: an inherited, established, or customary pattern of thought, action, or behavior (as a religious practice or a social custom); 2: the handing down of information, beliefs, and customs by word of mouth or by example from one generation to another without written instruction" (that is what American Indian tribes used to have for centuries and what made up their culture), *lore* – "a body of traditions relating to a person, institution, or place", *folklore* – "traditional customs, tales, sayings, dances, or art forms preserved among a people", *wisdom* – "1a: accumulated philosophic or scientific learning; ... 3: the teachings of the ancient wise men."[15] Regarding Native Americans, we may refer almost all of the notions to their stories as they have multiple functions. Literature itself does not fit this row: it is "writings in prose or verse; especially: writings having excellence of form or expression and expressing ideas of

---

[13] Webster Dictionary, [online] Available at: <http://www.webster.com> [Accessed 25 March 2002].
[14] See the definitions above.
[15] Webster Dictionary, [online] Available at: <http://www.webster.com> [Accessed 25 March 2002].

permanent or universal interest."[16] It can be referred to Native American writers and poets, but in this case it is rather a modern phenomenon and does not correspond to the older enumerated ones. We may also continue the list including religion, prayer, fairy tale and many more notions, but we base our research on mythology and the use of American Indian myths in their literature.

---

[16] Ibid.

1.2. Myth and Ritual. Storytelling

When we deal with American Indian mythology, we should remember that rituals and rites (ceremonial acts or actions) are not easily separated from mythology. Many rites are performed according to the models and patterns described in myths. Mythology and ritual are often interwoven as to be virtually inseparable. Holy stories, or story lines told through song, are common elements of ritual performances. The description of rites performed by mythic characters occur frequently in stories.[17] Even the name of the novel – *Ceremony* – suggests some rituals. The Night Chant in *House Made of Dawn* is also performed to complete the ritual of healing, and many other examples are found in both books. American Indian mythology "must be understood as existing only through its performance. Stories and rites are never frozen in Native American cultures as they are when published in books and pictures"[18] – that is what Leslie Marmon Silko tried to convey in her book. "Many myths and rituals are powerful precisely because they can be adapted and applied to so many situations"[19], and they will always live in

---
[17] Gill, S.D., Sullivan, I.F. Dictionary of Native American Mythology. NY – Oxford: Oxford University Press, 1992. P. XI.
[18] Ibid., p. XII.

American Indian cultures because they can be transformed to match the present-day needs.

Everything originated as a spoken word. Native American people

see the oral tradition as the means to establish their relationships between themselves, their past, and between themselves and nature. The language transporting the stories or the oral tradition has always been expressed through the use of storytellers who pass down cultural traditions from one generation to the next.[20]

"Language is also the marker of ethnic identity; it is not only a "spiritual force"[21], but also part of the ethnic self-identity of a person."[22]

Storytelling was more than important to preserve the knowledge of the tribe. Besides, it was part of social life.

---

[19] Ibid.
[20] The Role of Storytelling in Native American Cultures, [online] Available at: <http://homepages.uni-tuebingen.de/student/afra.korfmann/story.htm> [Accessed 21 March 2002].
[21] Moore, M. Genocide of the Mind: New Native American Writing. N.Y.: Thunder's Mouth Press/Nation Books, 2003. P. 111.
[22] Данчевская, О.Е. Слово как источник силы. Устные традиции в современной жизни североамериканских индейцев // Материалы 31 и 32 международных конференций ОИКС «Слово и/как власть: авторство и авторитет в американской культурной традиции» и «Америка реальная, воображаемая и виртуальная». – М.: Фак-т журналистики МГУ им. Ломоносова, 2006. С. 59-66. С. 61.

Traditionally, in American Indian cultures myths were passed from generation to generation orally. They had sacral information, were performed during ceremonies and during calendar rites, were interwoven into songs, ritual prayers and chants at all tribal gatherings, providing spiritual and physical survival. Rites with a spectacular performance of some myths were held to keep the balance and harmony in the world, for the continuation of the life of the community itself and all living things on the Earth. Naturally, the main role in all this was played by the Word, to which Native Americans have a particularly reverent attitude. [...] No wonder that in these cultures there is a special phenomenon called storytelling. Traditionally, storytellers enjoy great authority and respect, their stories are listened to by everyone, young and old alike, and their presence has long been considered an integral part of most American Indian celebrations and ceremonies.[23]

---

[23] Данчевская, О.Е. Американские индейцы в этнокультурной политике США конца 20 – начала 21 вв. М.: Прометей МПГУ, 2009. С. 103.

Western anthropology tends to treat such "narrations" as "myths" or "mythology", while the American Indians preferred the term "holy stories", or "stories", which, "according to the Native Americans' attitude to life contains much more than only words."[24] There are several important features about stories to be mentioned. Firstly, they include wisdom and traditions. Secondly, many of the American Indian people believe the stories about the origin of mankind and the holy creatures to be real. Studying the stories of different tribes, it may be seen that they are often repeating themselves or at least using the same fixed associations, as, for example, "coyote" – as a trickster and a storyteller, or "Spider-Woman" who is "responsible" for stories as well. "With her long legs and threads she is able to weave a story consisting of other "substories" and by this to create a web covering past, presence and future."[25] Although stories are part of the cultural background of a tribe, there are also stories which bear personal life experience – they are considered to be not less important. If we are to try to define the role of stories for American

---

[24] The Role of Storytelling in Native American Cultures, [online] Available at: <http://homepages.uni-tuebingen.de/student/afra.korfmann/story.htm> [Accessed 21 March 2002].
[25] Ibid.

Indians, it can be that of transporting thoughts, emotions, experience and knowledge. They also describe the history, life and behavior of a tribe.

Storytelling has several functions, the main ones being:
- description of the world order;
- reproduction of the history of a tribe (more frequently — in myths);
- explanation of the past and present events and phenomena;
- life descriptions of specific people;
- preservation and passing down of experience and knowledge;
- ritual one (being part of a ritual);
- secular one (e.g., entertaining stories), and others.[26]

When writing appeared, these stories were sometimes put onto paper, what was regarded both as an advantage and a disadvantage. On the one hand, this lets more people (even of different cultures) get acquainted with these myths and study them. In also helps preserve the stories, which can be especially important for smaller tribes. But at the same time with every new storyteller the myth was developed, some personal touch could be added, some new

---

[26] Данчевская, О.Е. Американские индейцы в этнокультурной политике США конца 20 – начала 21 вв. М.: Прометей МПГУ, 2009. С. 103-4.

features could be introduced, while written word is unchangeable and thus not "alive". Besides, writing down the stories leaves storytellers out, and though an American Indian would rather listen to them than read, such situations may interfere with the tradition. In any case, the form of the presentation does not influence the importance of the role of the Word, spoken or written, in American Indian conscience.

1.3. An Overview of Native American Mythology

Before studying some concrete myths and myth forms in the novels, it is necessary to have at least a general idea about Native American mythology and its peculiarities. We would only state the major notions relevant to our subject, and we want to start with religion as it is tightly connected with mythology, and in Native American case it is especially true. Ch.L. Heyrman gives three generalizations about American Indian religion which fit any tribe's world-outlook. These generalizations are (we will quote them):

1. First, at the time of European contact, all but the simplest indigenous cultures in North America had developed coherent religious systems that included cosmologies – creation myths, transmitted orally from one generation to the next, which purported to explain how those societies had come into being.

2. Second, most native peoples worshiped an all-powerful, all-knowing Creator or "Master Spirit" (a being that assumed a variety of forms and both genders). They also venerated or placated a host of lesser supernatural entities, including

an evil god who dealt out disaster, suffering, and death.

3. Third and finally, the members of most tribes believed in the immortality of the human soul and an afterlife, the main feature of which was the abundance of every good thing that made earthly life secure and pleasant.[27]

Obviously, there is a lot in common between such religious concept and that of Christianity (as well as other religions). Maybe that was one of the reasons why the new, European religion was assimilated into and even developed by the tribes (though they transformed it to fit their reality). According to B.A. Robinson, Natives today follow many spiritual traditions: many Native families today have been devout Christians for generations. Others, practically in the Southwest, have retained their aboriginal traditions more or less intact. Most follow a personal faith that combines traditional and Christian elements. Pan-Indianism is a recent and growing movement which encourages a return to traditional beliefs, and seeks to create a common Native religion. The Native American Church is a continuation of the ancient Peyote Religion which

---

[27] Heyrman, Ch.L. Native American Religion in Early America, [online] Available at: <http://www.nhc.rtp.nc.us:8080/tserve/eighteen/ekeyinfo/natrel.htm> [Accessed 30 November 2001].

had used a cactus with psychedelic properties called peyote for about 10,000 years.[28] It is easily understood that though the religions of particular tribes may differ, there are many similarities.

Here are some of the similarities in religion and ritual among the tribes that are worth mentioning.

Deity: a common concept is that of a dual divinity: a Creator who is responsible for the creation of the world and is recognized in religious rituals and prayers on the one hand, and a mythical individual, a hero or a trickster, who teaches culture, proper behavior and provides sustenance to the tribe. There are also spirits which control the weather, spirits which interact with humans, and others who inhabit the underworld. Simultaneously the Creator and the spirits may be perceived as a single spiritual force.

Creation: individual tribes have different stories of Creation. One set of themes found in some tribes describes that in the beginning the world was populated by many people. Most were subsequently transformed into animals. Natives thus feel a close bond with animals because of

---

[28] Robinson, B.A. Native American Spirituality, [online] Available at: <http://www.religioustolerance.org/nataspir.htm> [Accessed 13 February 2002].

their shared human ancestry. Dogs are excluded from this relationship. This bond is shown in the frequent rituals in which animal behavior is simulated. Each species has its master; for example, the deer have a master deer who is larger than all the others. The master of humans is the Creator.

Emergence of the tribe: this is a concept found extensively in the Southwest. The universe is believed to consist of many dark, underground layers through which the humans had to climb. They emerged into the present world through a small hole in the ground – the world's navel (sipapu). For example, the Navajo myths describe the people constantly climbing from the lowest (the first) to the present (the fifth) world. Other tribes believe that their ancestors have been present in North America as far back as there were humans.

Sacred texts: many tribes have complex forms of writing. Other tribes have preserved their spiritual beliefs as an oral tradition (this point is very important for our research, especially in the part describing the role of storytelling for the Natives).

Shamans: though the term "shaman" takes its origins in Siberia, it is often used by anthropologists throughout the world to refer to Aboriginal healers. The term used by Native

Americans themselves is "medicine man". "They are not only endowed with the ability and power to heal (with the help of rituals, herbs, spells, etc.), but also carry the secret knowledge of their people, which distinguishes them among others, because knowledge, according to a number of myths, is the main source of supernatural power."[29]

The very concept of "medicine man" can also be translated as "holy man", which is absolutely consistent with the idea of such an individual, in whose life there is no strict distinction between religious, ritual and medical practices. This is also due to the fact that many of the shaman's rituals are related. Thus, medicine men have power over diseases, to some extent over the order of things in the world surrounding the tribe (as intermediaries between higher powers and the people), are often endowed with the gift of prophecy, and also occupy a central place in rituals, ceremonies and preservation and transferring of the spiritual heritage of the tribe using all this power for the benefit of their society.[30]

---

[29] Данчевская, О.Е. Сверхъестественная власть и её носители в мифах о Первотворении индейцев Юго-Запада США // Антропология власти: Феномен власти в аборигенной Америке. М.: Наука, 2006. С. 428-438. С. 434.

A medicine man usually has several helping spirits which may be encouraged to occupy his body during public lodge ceremonies. Drum beating and chanting aid this process (drums are very frequently used in American Indian ceremonies; in our study they will be mentioned during the performance of the Night Chant and the festival in *House Made of Dawn* and in several other places). The spirits are then asked to depart and perform the needed acts. Other times, medicine men enter into a trance and traverse the underworld or go great distances in this world to seek lost possessions or healing.

Vision Quest: young boys before or at puberty are encouraged to enter into a period of fasting, meditation and physical challenge. Girls are not usually eligible for a quest. The young man separates himself from the tribe and goes to a wilderness area. The goal is to receive a vision that will guide his development for the rest of his life. They also seek to acquire a guardian spirit who will be close and supportive for their lifetime.

Renewal Celebrations: the ritual calendar of agrarian tribes is strictly divided into seasonal rituals which are connected with natural cycles; the main purpose is to keep the balance and cyclicality of life. Other tribes have the Sun Dance which is perceived as a replay of the original

---

[30] Ibid.

creation. Its name is a mistranslation of the Lakota *sun gazing dance*, but names can differ. It fulfilled many religious purposes: to give thanks to the Creator, to pray for the renewal of the people and earth, to promote health, etc. It also gave an opportunity for people to socialize and renew friendships with other groups.

Sweat Lodge: this is a structure which generates hot moist air, similar to a Finnish sauna. It is used for rituals of purification, for spiritual renewal and for healing, for education of the youth, etc. A sweat lodge may be a small structure made of a frame of saplings, covered with skins, canvas or blanket. A depression is dug in the center into which hot rocks are positioned. Water is thrown on the rocks to create steam. A small flap opening is used to regulate the temperature. As many as a dozen people can be accommodated in some lodges.

Hunting ceremonies: these involve the ritual treatment of a bear or other animal after its killing during a successful hunt. The goal is to appease its spirit and convince other animals to be willing to be killed in the future. Hunting rituals are described quite in detail in both books, mentioning deer and bear hunts.[31]

---

[31] Information in this chapter is partially taken from: Native American, [online] Available at: <http://www.bright.net/~jimsjems/native.html> [Accessed 10 February 2002].

Religion gives birth to mythology, or vice versa – it might be one of those rhetorical questions which will never be answered. In case of Native Americas, it is difficult to differentiate between these two notions, but we find mythology more overwhelming and general.

American Indian philosophy is the world-outlook of a parish where a person sees himself as part of the surrounding world and, consequently, does not oppose himself to nature (which he has to subordinate to himself!), but feels he is kindred with it: Mother Earth, Father Sun, Granny Moon, Corn, Spider, River – they all are live, "inspired" creatures, whom one should respect and by no way destroy in order not to break the balance of the whole (the Universe) and thus oneself. This is a fraternity culture with visible social structures, where power does not mean domination, where there is a place for men and women, for the old and for the young.[32]

There is no strict hierarchy of gods or spirits in American Indian mythology. The personification of supernatural beings is very weakly expressed. The *four parts of the world*, the *four elements*

---

[32] Бауэр, В., Дюмоц, И., Головин, С. Энциклопедия символов. М.: КРОН-ПРЕСС, 1995. С. 84.

(earth, fire, wind, water), with the symbols of colors and various objects and natural phenomena attributed to them, are widely used. "The combination of the four parts of the world is the symbol of finality and unity of the world, it is closely connected with the idea of the cyclicality of everything."[33] Associations with *numbers* are quite similar among all American Indians, the most important number being four.[34]

Color for Native Americans "plays a very important part as it has deep symbolic and sacral meaning and is used everywhere — in mythology, religion, art, daily life"; "the general color palette of different tribes is the same and universal, and it consists of only six basic colors (white, black, red, yellow, blue and green)".[35]

All natural phenomena possess some magic *power* ("*medicine*") which does not only

---

[33] Токарев, С.А. (ред.). Мифы народов мира: Энциклопедия в 2 т. М.: Советская Энциклопедия, 1991. Т.1. С. 512.

[34] Danchevskaya, O.Y. Numbers in American Indian Mythology. Native Leadership: Past, Present and Future. Proceedings of the Eleventh Native American Symposium. Durant, Oklahoma: Southeastern Oklahoma State University, 2017. - in press

[35] Данчевская, О.Е. Цветовая символика в культурах североамериканских индейцев // Город и урбанизм в американской культуре. Материалы XXXVII международной конференции Российского общества по изучению культуры США. М.: Фак-т журналистики МГУ, 2014. С. 264-280. С. 278.

determine a spirit or a deity but also the whole world and any supernatural ability.

A whole series of concepts related to the sphere of the sacred, such as, for example, authority, strength, knowledge, magic, etc., are expressed in American Indian myths by only this word. The opinion of the authors of the *Dictionary of Native American Mythology* S. Gill and I. Sullivan perfectly confirms this idea: "...Native American religions can be understood in terms of power. To know stories, prayers, and songs; to practice ritual; to have visions and dreams; to be able to call upon guardian spirits and helping spirits — these things mean power; they allow one to live a meaningful life. In the most general terms, power is denoted by the English term *medicine*[36] (magic), representing something that exists on the verge of the two worlds — the mythological (otherworldly) and the real (our) ones.[37]

---

[36] Gill, S.D., Sullivan, I.F. Dictionary of Native American Mythology. NY – Oxford: Oxford University Press, 1992. P. 242.

[37] Данчевская, О.Е. Сверхъестественная власть и её носители в мифах о Первотворении индейцев Юго-Запада США // Антропология власти: Феномен власти в аборигенной Америке. М.: Наука, 2006. С. 428-438. С. 428.

Almost every tribe has a *creation myth* (it цas already been mentioned above). Emergence and migration myths are very characteristic of Native American tribes, as well as the myths about their acquiring of wonderful talismans and relics. Rather known is the *twins myth* in its different variations – it is met in the mythologies of all American Indians, its both motifs being used: as brothers-antagonists and as brothers-creators. In full accordance with the ideas of C. Levi-Strauss, the mythical twins "symbolize the counterbalancing principles of good and evil"[38]. P. Radin called the twin myth "basic" in aboriginal America because of its wide distribution and importance "from Canada to the South of South America and from the Pacific to the Atlantic Oceans."[39] The most common "tandem" twin motif appears in the fact that "twin brothers in North American myths (usually the sons of the Sun) go to their father for a wonderful weapon, free the land from drought and numerous monsters, descend into the underground world, taking people from it, or obtaining necessary talismans and bequeathing them to the people".[40]

---

[38] Cirlot, J.E. A Dictionary of Symbols. London: Routledge, 1971. P. 356.
[39] Radin, P. The Basic Myth of North American Indians // Eranos-Jahrbuch: Der Mensch und die Mythische Welt, Band XVII (1949). Zurich: Rhein-Verlag, 1950. P. 359-419. P. 359.

Widely spread is the zoomorphic (more rarely faceless or anthropomorphic at the same time) personage who unites the features of a culture hero and the creator of the world, often along with the functions of a malefactor, a wise fool-*trickster* able of transformations. By the definition of Paul Radin, the trickster is "admittedly the oldest of all figures in American Indian mythology, probably in all mythologies"; he is "everything to man — god, animal, human being, hero, buffoon, he who was before good and evil, denier, affirmer, destroyer and creator" who "knows neither good nor evil yet he is responsible for both"; "He possesses no values, moral or social, [...] yet through his actions all values come into being".[41] In the image of the trickster contradictory beginnings are united, which mirror primeval syncretism of beliefs about the good and the evil. As culture hero he is the thief of the fire, the inventor of crafts, the savior of people, the winner over monsters, and so on.[42]

Native American mythology and religion

---

[40] Ващенко, А.В. Суд Париса. Сравнительная мифология в культуре и цивилизации. М.: ФИЯиР МГУ, 2008. С. 60.

[41] Radin, P. The Trickster. A Study in Native American Mythology. – N.Y.: Philosophical Library, 1956. PP. 164; 169; IX.

[42] Токарев, С.А. (ред.). Мифы народов мира: Энциклопедия в 2 т. М.: Советская Энциклопедия, 1991. Т.1. С. 514.

cannot be studied in isolation from *animism* and *totemism*. American Indians believe that not only animals, birds, fish and other fauna have a soul, but also plants. E.B. Tylor mentions object souls, the belief in which was especially strong among the Algonquin. In other words, the whole world around is animated. [...] No wonder that in myths every animal and even insect represents a separate nation, because if all have soul, both humans and all living beings should be related in a certain way. "The savage quite seriously speaks about the dead and living animals as of dead and living people".[43] Reasoning from this concept, it is easy to understand why animals became totems and protectors for American Indians. [...] It accounts for the presence of *hunting rites* when the hunter asks the killed animal for forgiveness and gives gifts to it, as "the souls of animals respond to human actions punishing people for pointless destruction of animals and thanking them for showing kindness to them"[44].[45]

---

[43] Тэйлор, Э. Первобытная культура: В 2 кн. М.: ТЕРРА – Книжный клуб, 2009. Т.2. С. 48.
[44] Кремо, М.А. Деволюция человека: Ведическая альтернатива теории Дарвина, [online] Available at: <http://bookz.ru/authors/maikl-kremo/devoluci_690/1-

A popular motif is that of the transformation of humans into animals and journeys to the other world. In the myths of agricultural tribes (the Iroquois, the Algonkin, the Pueblo and others) an important place is given to the deities who personify useful *plants* (mainly maize). Often individuals or whole tribes go for help to spiritual powers of nature. In this case individuals may use private prayers or sacrifices of valuable items (furs, tobacco, food, etc.), and entire communities usually seek "divine assistance to ensure a successful hunt, a good harvest, or victory in warfare" with *shamans*, whom they believe

> to have acquired supernatural powers through visions. These uncommon abilities included predicting the future and influencing the weather – matters of vital interest to whole tribes – but shamans might also assist individuals by interpreting dreams and curing or causing outbreaks of witchcraft.[46]

---

devoluci_690.html> [Accessed September 20 2015].
[45] Danchevskaya, O.Y. Concept of Soul among North American Indians. Where No One Else Has Gone Before: Proceedings of the Ninth Native American Symposium. Durant, Oklahoma: Southeastern Oklahoma State University, 2012. P. 89-96. (Also available online at: <http://homepages.se.edu/nas/files/2013/03/NAS-2011-Proceedings-Danchevskaya.pdf>)
[46] The Role of Storytelling in Native American Cultures, [online] Available at: <http://homepages.uni-

Totem poles (mainly on the Northwest Coast) also help in many situations. They often reach gigantic proportions and have figures representing the animals from which human prominent families have descended carved into them. "In this area's mythology, during the primordial era all beings were animals, some of whom removed their animal forms to reveal a human form".[47] Such poles are used in *ceremonies* (during the Winter Ceremonial Season), usually accompanied by animal masks. An interesting description and classification of totem poles of the Haida is given in Alexander Vaschenko's book "A Pole Supporting the World...": "It is important to realize that the poles are not altars or idols, but symbols of the status of the house, clan, chief, and usually are not subject to renewal — you can only put new ones in honor of the same and new names, clans and events."[48]

Masks in general are very popular with any ancient culture. They are used on religious occasions. They are often considered living beings

---

tuebingen.de/student/afra.korfmann/story.htm> [Accessed 21 March 2002].

[47] Gill, S.D., Sullivan, I.F. Dictionary of Native American Mythology. NY – Oxford: Oxford University Press, 1992. P. 306.

[48] Ващенко, А.В. Столб, подпирающий мир: традиция и современность на Хайда Гвай. Владения гитксанов. Ногинск: АНАЛИТИКА РОДИС, 2012. С. 15.

and hold the power to cure as well as to entertain. With the help of masks one can communicate with the spiritual world and the world of the dead. "With each type of masks, myths are associated with the purpose of explaining their legendary or supernatural origin and substantiating their role in ritual, economics, social life..."[49]

Though the features that we have enumerated are common to all American Indian tribes, the mythology of each one contains its particular heroes and aspects and is very rich in symbols.

As already mentioned, everything is treated as live, that is why there is such a number of symbolic signs and personifications (which are very different from the mythologies of the ancient European peoples). These symbols can be those of the universe and the contents of the world, of natural phenomena, animals, plants, and many more... Here we will describe shortly the most widely used ones.

The *universe*, the *earth* is usually the major symbol of Native American mythology and is usually visualized as a figure with four equal parts or elements – the four parts of the world. The

---

[49] Леви-Строс, К. Путь масок. М.: Республика, 2000. С. 25.

rock, the *mountain*, and the *pyramid* as its form are very important: a stone means a long-lasting stability, the initial and the most ancient substance, the symbol of the beginning of the beginning. The *tree*, the *pole*, and the *cross* deal with the creation: a stick became a great tree, and all human tribes could rest under its crown. This tree, the first tree of the world, the father of the universe and the man, has a more than a thousand years' tradition and a divine predestination like stone structures. "The image of Arbor Mundi (the world tree) is especially widespread. [...] By its vertical, the tree unites three worlds — the underworld of the dead, the past; the middle (contemporary) world of living beings; and the heavenly world of the future."[50]

The *sun* and the *moon* are met in the mythologies of all peoples of our planet. "Of all celestial bodies, the sun is the most commonly personified in Native American stories. Not surprisingly, the sun is often identified as the creator of the world"[51], while "the moon is the most mysterious of all the bodies in the sky" and is an "important co-creator with the Sun Father"[52].

---

[50] Ващенко, А.В. Суд Париса. Сравнительная мифология в культуре и цивилизации. М.: ФИЯиР МГУ, 2008. С. 36-7.

[51] Gill, S.D., Sullivan, I.F. Dictionary of Native American Mythology. NY – Oxford: Oxford University Press, 1992. P. 290.

[52] Ibid., pp. 194-5.

"Solar myths are the most common ones in world mythology. However, the myths of North American Indians "are of the greatest interest because of the ingenuity of the legends and their diversity"[53], as well as because of their significant impact on the religious and ceremonial life both in the past and in the present."[54] In Native Americans' view, the sun, as well as the earth and the whole universe, are combined and coincide with the top deity.

> According to [some — O.D.] American Indian beliefs, the Sun and the Moon are one and the same luminary, but they see it from different sides. They both make the sun, but it, in its turn, can be day and night one, the Moon being the "night" sun. If the Sun is fire, the Moon is water.[55]

The sun is also associated with light and power. This shows the role of the four elements, which are ascribed to the majority if not all things.

Water and *rain* are vital for life, and ancient American Indians, for whom the main values were

---

[53] Олкотт, У.Т. Мифы о солнце. М.: ЗАО Центрполиграф, 2013. С. 8.
[54] Данчевская, О.Е. Солнце в мифологии и жизни индейцев Северной Америки // Феномен творческой личности в культуре. Материалы VI международной конференции. М.: МГУ, 2014. С. 36-46. С. 38.
[55] Бауэр, В., Дюмоц, И., Головин, С. Энциклопедия символов. М.: КРОН-ПРЕСС, 1995. С. 92.

health and food, knew it perfectly well – all this depends on water. That's why there are even special rites to call upon the rain, especially in case of drought, and the most beloved gem by Native Americans — turquoise — was also "the most important stone of medicine men capable of causing rain" [56]. Water is usually pictured as a series of
wavy lines one under another.

The *bird* often goes together with or close to the *serpent*, and sometimes even the feathered serpent figures in the myths. One of the most important deities is *Thunderbird*. The image of the bird Ketsal', or Ketsal'koatl' (more common in Mesoamerica), appeared from the merging of a bird and a snake; it is a general name for any god-creator. Ketsal' is considered to be the most beautiful bird. "A feathered serpent used to signify water and fertile growth of all plants under the influence of the rain ... the symbol of the sky in general."[57] Thus, in Ketsal'koatl', the most

---

[56] Danchevskaya, O.Y. Turquoise in the Life of American Indians. Images, Imaginations, and Beyond. Proceedings of the Eighth Native American Symposium. Ed. by Mark B. Spencer. Durant, Oklahoma: Southeastern Oklahoma State University, 2010. P. 144-149. P. 146. (Also available online at: <http://homepages.se.edu/nas/files/2013/03/NAS-2009-Proceedings-Danchevskaya.pdf>)

[57] Бауэр, В., Дюмоц, И., Головин, С. Энциклопедия символов. М.: КРОН-ПРЕСС, 1995. С. 97.

popular of all the deities of ancient American Indians, different deities merged into one.

An important place is occupied by the *bear* (almost in all mythologies, the symbol of the Creator), who is "considered to be a powerful ally in healing" and "is revered in hunting practices"[58]; the *serpent* (the symbol of the earth) and the *eagle* (the symbol of the sun), who can also appear as Thunderbird; the *bison* with the tribes of the prairies; the *wolf*, the *dog*, the *fox* and other animals with the Plains tribes are considered to be the founders of war unions. There are some stories about the *hummingbird* in Native American mythology; they will be described below. In general, there are very many – if not all – animals represented in Native American mythologies, which usually share the same or similar features with different tribes, though there may be exceptions. Almost all of the above-mentioned symbols are used in the novels.

Now just a few words about some typical figures of the Pueblo mythology (the ones which will be met in the analyzed novels). All the deities described in the previous chapter function in it, too, that is why we will only widen the range a

---

[58] Gill, S.D., Sullivan, I.F. Dictionary of Native American Mythology. NY – Oxford: Oxford University Press, 1992. P. 23.

little. *Clouds* are associated with rain and the fertilization of the earth. "Humans who live good lives become clouds or Cloud People after death". "If properly remembered and fed, the dead serve the living as clouds and rain bringers, bringing rain and life".[59] *Yellow Woman*, or *Corn Woman*, is a figure in many stories; she takes "a wide range of identities, including bride, witch, chief's daughter, bear woman, and ogress"[60], which shows the importance of maize for the Pueblos like for all Native Americans. As all other tribes, the Pueblos have their *emergence and migration myth*. "Origin stories usually begin with the world already in existence, the people living in the worlds below this one. They emerge, often led by heroic figures, onto this world and begin journeys (migrations) to the south or east in search of suitable homes."[61] A lot of times the people stop and settle, but due to various reasons they have to move on until they find their final location.

As mentioned above, *hummingbirds* are rather popular.

> The Pueblo Indians have hummingbird dances and use hummingbird feathers in rituals to bring rain. Pueblo shamans use

---

[59] Gill, S.D., Sullivan, I.F. Dictionary of Native American Mythology. NY – Oxford: Oxford University Press, 1992. P. 23. P. 49.
[60] Ibid., p. 358.
[61] Ibid., p. 244.

hummingbirds as couriers to send gifts to the Great Mother who lives beneath the earth. To many of the Pueblo the hummingbird is a tobacco bird. In one myth Hummingbird gets smoke from Caterpillar, the guardian of the tobacco plant. Hummingbird brings smoke to the shamans so they can purify the earth.[62]

This exact myth can be found among others in the novels, this tiny bird acting with a number of various animals, insects, birds, plants, deities, and spirits. Many other stories are woven through this framework. The world below is mentioned in the poem *Ceremony* in L.M. Silko's novel. Special attention has been paid to the Pueblo mythology because both protagonists are Pueblos, but in the novels under study stories and mythology of other tribes are also used, especially in *House Made of Dawn* by N.S. Momaday. We will not stop on every tribe's mythology because on the level of our research the knowledge of the most general aspects of Native American mythology with occasional close-ups further on is sufficient.

---

[62] Native American Mythology, [online] Available at: <http://portalproductions.com/h/native_american.htm> [Accessed 24 February 2002].

Chapter 2. Native American Literature

Fiction as a form of art arose on the basis of oral-poetic folk art which keeps, accumulates and transmits aesthetic, spiritual, moral, philosophical, social and other values. Only with the coming of the Europeans to the continent certain such works began to be written down by them (the first cases date back to the 1600s). Those were collections of myths, speeches of American Indian chiefs (for example, the famous Chief Seattle's speech of 1854), and later also biographies and stories of Native Americans written down on dictation (like the already classical work *Black Elk Speaks* written down by J.G. Neihardt in 1932). However, if truly American Indian authors appeared in the 18th — beginning of the 19th centuries, such as E. Boudinot, those were only singular cases at that time, the first attempts, which is valuable in itself. In 1854 the first book written by an American Indian was published — *The Life and Adventures of Joaquín Murieta: The Celebrated California Bandit* by J.R. Ridge. Then followed the first novel by a Native American woman — *Wynema, a Child of the Forest* by S.A. Callahan, published in 1891. At the end of the 19th century The Red Man's Rebuke (1893) made the author famous — the chief of Potawatomi tribe S. Pokagon, who wrote several books during his lifetime. From the beginning of the 20th century the topics of race and gender relations could be traced in E. Pauline Johnson's (1913) and Mourning Dove's (1927) books. In the novels by J.J. Mathews (1934) and D'Arcy McNickle (1936) the question which became one of the central in Native American literature was formed more clearly — the one about the destiny of half-bloods.[63]

The turning point for the United States in the cultural and political terms were the 1960s and 1970s. It was then that the term "ethnic literature" appeared in American literary criticism. During this period there was an increase in the self-awareness of national minorities, which manifested itself in the emergence and active work of various organizations defending human rights. This is also the time that American critics called "Great

---

[63] Данчевская, О.Е. Американские индейцы в этнокультурной политике США конца 20 – начала 21 вв. М.: Прометей МПГУ, 2009. С. 112-3.

Awakening" in relation to the "color" population and the "Indian Renaissance" in relation to Native Americans. It is interesting that in the aforementioned years the process of the formation of ethnic literatures has acquired global dimensions. Leading literary critics agree that their main feature as of relatively young literatures is the active appeal of the authors to folklore traditions, the genetic core of which is a myth; [...] in many Native American novels [...] the heroes gradually come to understand the need to return to the origins of their culture[64].

So, with the new freedom for Native Americans, new phenomena appeared, Native American writers and poets being among them. Some of those authors became well-known and even got prestigious literary awards. The Pulitzer Prize awarded in 1969 to N.S. Momaday for his novel *House Made of Dawn* was something like a sensation: the first award given to a Native American writer. Before, there was another award for works about American Indians, but they were

---

[64] Данчевская, О.Е. Индейское наследие в американской культуре // Сборник материалов Международной конференции «Язык, культура, речевое общение»: К 85-летию профессора Марка Яковлевича Блоха. В двух частях. М.: Прометей, 2009. Часть 1. С. 170-173. С. 171.

written by the whites. The greater part of American Indian writers depict subjects close to them – the lives of different tribes and their representatives, their relations with the white world, their experiences...

Native American ethnic literature is notable for its specific features. The themes, ideas, plots, heroes, places of action, author's manner of presentation, style and even the language, full of words and expressions taken from the native language of these or those tribes, will eloquently testify that these artistic creations have come from under the pen of American Indian writers. They deeply reveal the nature, customs and morals, beliefs, aspirations and ideals of Native Americans. Special attention should be paid to myths skillfully woven into the canvas of works, for it was this epic genre that was most developed in the oral folk art of American Indians. Methods of their transfer are very diverse. The myth can be presented in its pure form or sound like a retelling in the mouth of the hero, it can be a synthesis of the myth itself and artistic fiction, and at times be transmitted through the prism of the author's perception... It is like a plot inside the plot, but always subject to the main idea of the artist and pursues specific goals — to more fully reveal the character of the literary hero, understand the motives of his actions, searches and experiences. That is why myths can be called with certainty one of the most important components of the works of American Indian writers.[65]

There is a number of mythological poems and songs in such books, what shares them out from other literature and makes distinct even graphically (though some white writers go to the American Indian topic more and more often and start to adopt Native American style). American Indians manifested their writing talent both in prose and poetry, and it is even hard to say which part of literature has more prominent Native American authors.

We will dwell on the analysis of the novels by only two writers, who, perhaps, received the greatest fame and who are at the forefront of modern American Indian prose – N.S. Momaday and L.M. Silko.

---

[65] Данчевская, О.Е. Мифы североамериканских индейцев в романах «Церемония» Л.М. Силко и «Дом, из рассвета сотворенный» Н.Скотта Момадэя // Актуальные проблемы исследования англоязычных литератур: международный сборник научных статей. Классики и современники. Минск: РИВШ, 2008. Вып. 7. С. 174-183. С. 174.

Chapter 3. An Overview of American Indian History

Mythology of any people as part of its culture has always been connected with its history, that is why we find it important to give at least a brief overview of the history of Native Americans. Nobody can say exactly when the first inhabitants appeared on the American continents, but everyone agrees it was thousands of years ago.[66] Before 1492, when Columbus discovered America, the tribes had a rich culture manifested not only in mythology but also in architecture, artcraft, rituals, etc. Ancient remains of that culture are still found all over the continents. There were warrior tribes and peaceful ones; sometimes unions were made, like the Iroquois Confederacy. Many tribes migrated from one place to another for various reasons, and that is mirrored in their myths. But then the colonists came and brought crucial changes with them. Some of the tribes were very friendly, but the majority were or became hostile because the

---

[66] "According to the most common theory, America was inhabited by natives of northeast Asia, who migrated to the new continent via the isthmus through the Bering Strait about 25-30 thousand years ago." (Данчевская, О.Е. Американские индейцы в этнокультурной политике США конца 20 – начала 21 вв. М.: Прометей МПГУ, 2009. С. 26.)

white men brought bad luck: new diseases to which the natives had had no immunity, slavery, wars, robbery, invasions... Within a short period of time the land which had initially belonged to American Indians was taken by the colonists, and the aborigines were pushed away from what used to be their homes. That gave birth to a series of cruel wars, but as the whites had modern arms and outnumbered the Natives, American Indians lost their battle for freedom. The proud people were suppressed. "It is one thing for immigrants to conform to their new country, and entirely another for indigenous peoples to submit to the conqueror. The designers of manifest destiny could tolerate other cultures, even those that had welcomed them to these shores."[67] From the first years of the colonization of North America, the new settlers developed different policies and attitudes towards the native population, the most peaceful of which was to "civilize" it. For this purpose they strongly relied on religion, but though missionaries formally supported Native Americans, in fact the former helped to subjugate the latter maintaining the colonizers' ideas of assimilation. To justify its violence, the Church

---

[67] Ryan, J.B. Listening to Native Americans // Listening: Journal of Religion and Culture, Vol. 31, No.1 Winter 1996 pp. 24-36, [online] Available at: <http://www.op.org/DomCentral/library/native.htm> [Accessed 06 March 2002].

officially regarded the natives as a lower race, "noble savages"[68], and saw its mission in "civilizing" them.

Some groups converted to Christianity in vain hope to be saved by the strong God of the newcomers from unknown diseases, but their conversion was only partial, with Native Americans still practicing their traditional beliefs, mostly secretly due to the long history of cruel suppression of such beliefs.

Though physically they were conquered, spiritually they continued to live in their would and did not want to become Christians, but had no choice.

> The European invasion and the cultural decline of aboriginal culture caused by it led to the appearing of a series of messiah teachings, prophecies in the Indian environment, where traditional mythological views were connected in strange variations with some dogmas of Christianity.[69]

---

[68] For more information on the stereotypes of Native Americans, see: Danchevskaya, O.Y. Stereotyping American Indians. Sixty-Seven Nations and Counting: Proceedings of the Seventh Native American Symposium. Ed. by Mark B. Spencer and Rachel Tudor. Durant, Oklahoma: Southeastern Oklahoma State University, 2008. P.112-117. (Also available online at: <http://homepages.se.edu/nas/files/2013/03/NAS-2007-Proceedings-Danchevskaya.pdf>)

[69] Токарев, С.А. (ред.). Мифы народов мира: Энциклопедия в 2 т. М.: Советская Энциклопедия, 1991.

The whites were rejoiced, but in vain: inside, the culture and its rituals remained, though sometimes transformed under the influence of Christianity and the numerous prohibitions to practise them. It cost a lot, as "Native spirituality was suppressed by the US and Canadian governments. Spiritual leaders ran the risk of jail sentences of up to 30 years for simply practicing their rituals."[70] In 1883, Congress passed Religious Crimes Code which aimed at banning all Native American religious practices and severely punished those who disobeyed. This code was fractionally revoked only in 1934 by Indian Reorganisation Act, but officially the end to religious discrimination was ended in 1978 by American Indian Religious Freedom Act. Still, it was not fully effective, and only in 1994 another Act solved many of the problems.

Today in the USA we have a number of traditional beliefs and even a Native American Church (founded in 1918), but they have been seriously influenced by Christianity and have become syncretic. This influence can be easily traced in Native American mythology.

T.1. C. 515.

[70] Robinson, B.A. Native American Spirituality, [online] Available at:
<http://www.religioustolerance.org/nataspir.htm>
[Accessed 13 February 2002].

One of the ways of interaction between the whites and American Indians were the treaties. In the USA, "between 1778, when the first treaty was signed with the Dalawares, and 1868, when the final one was completed with the Nez Perces, there were 367 ratified Indian treaties and 6 more whose status is questionable. In addition, a considerable number of treaties that were signed by the Indian chiefs and the federal commissioners were never ratified by the Senate and the president."[71] In Canada, the treaty policy lasted from 1850 to 1923. Sadly, a great number of those treaties were broken (which in 1972 led to the Trail of Broken Treaties protest, the aim of which was rallying Native Americans, a public statement of their troubles and the request from the government to correct the mistakes it had made, but the desired results were not achieved[72]).

With the expansion of their settlements, the colonists realized that Native Americans were an obstacle for them, and thus, with Indian Removal Act of 1830, reservations officially appeared – a political act to "save" and "protect" those peoples,

---

[71] Prucha, F.P. American Indian Treaties: The History of a Political Anomaly. Berkeley etc.: Univ. of California Press, 1997. P. 1.

[72] Prucha, F.P. The Indians in American Society: From the Revolutionary War to the Present. Berkeley etc.: Univ. of California Press, 1985. P. 412.

which was in fact an act of protecting themselves from the American Indian threat by localizing them on restricted territories. There were vain attempts to confront such discrimination, but they all failed. Probably the most notorious one was *Cherokee Nation vs. Georgia* court case in 1831 which resulted in the deportation of the whole nation to Oklahoma. It got the name of the Trail of Tears (1838-39), during which 1/4 of the tribe died...[73]

Missionaries lay the foundation of the first schools for Native Americans that were to become another tool in the process of their assimilation. After a few unsuccessful variants of such schools, in 1878 the U.S. government introduced boarding schools based on the ideas of R.H. Pratt whose goal was to "kill the Indian and save the man". Native American children were forcibly removed from their families on reservations despite their parents' protests and sent to boarding schools where any manifestation of their culture was forbidden. Some children ran away, some died, others continued to secretly speak their language and practise some traditions, but in almost six decades of its existence such education policy broke many souls.

---

[73] Bordewich, F.M. Killing the White Man's Indian: Reinventing Native Americans at the End of the Twentieth Century. N.Y.: Anchor Books, 1997. P. 45-7.

The US and Canadian governments instituted policies to force Natives onto reservations and to encourage them to become assimilated into the majority culture. During the middle decades of the 20th century, whole generations of children were kidnapped, forcibly confined in residential schools, and abused physically, sexually and emotionally.[74]

Another invention brought from Europe – alcohol – proved to be destructive for the conquered and insulted people. Many of them got despaired, became alcoholics, degraded… Even when racism was fought against, American Indians were not given equal rights; they were still not treated as equals for a long time. A study for the Royal Commission on Bilingualism and Biculturalism of Canada held in the mid-1960s may serve as an example: it showed that the income of Amerindians was ranked fourteenth out of the 14 main ethnic groups in Quebec. The situation in the USA was not much better. It was only in 1924 in the USA and in 1947 (retroactively in 1956) in Canada that Native Americans were given full citizenship and the right to vote. The issue of racism seems to be one of eternal issues

---

[74] Robinson, B.A. Native American Spirituality, [online] Available at: <http://www.religioustolerance.org/nataspir.htm> [Accessed 13 February 2002].

of humankind. So, some Native American families have the problem of mixed identity; for instance, the mother is Native American but the father is white. They live on reservation but are not really accepted as "real" Native Americans because of their white inheritance (thus, racism also lives among the tribal members themselves). A great deal was committed against American Indians, with and without such a purpose. Some suicidologists even believe that the extremely high suicide rate among Natives is due to the suppression of their religion and culture by the Federal Governments. Among other misdeeds may be mentioned the Federal Government's attempt to wipe out tribal identities through laws that forbade tribal religious ceremonies, the speaking of the tribal languages, and the removal of American Indian children off the reservations to be educated in white American schools. Even in case of treaties that are made between two theoretically sovereign entities (as many tribes have managed to obtain self-government rights), one party to the treaty cannot legally abrogate it. That does not mean that treaties do not get broken – as it was mentioned above, the U.S. Government broke treaties with various groups of American Indians repeatedly, but at least in the last few decades it is trying not to repeat these particular actions of the past.

Mainly owing to continuous resistance to suppression, Native Americans managed to preserve a greater part of their culture. Still, some of it was irrevocably lost due to the aggressive policies of the colonizers...

Only in the recent decades many steps have been made to reconcile with the native population and to try to smooth the harm done to them. One of such steps was taken in November, 1987, when

> on the occasion of the second hundred anniversary year of the United States Constitution, church leaders of the Pacific Northwest issued "A Public Declaration to the Tribal Councils and Traditional Spiritual Leaders of the Indian and Eskimo Peoples of the Pacific Northwest". This declaration contained a formal apology for participation in the destruction of traditional Native American spiritual practices.
>
> The remainder of the Northwest clergy apology is a pledge of support to uphold the American Religious Freedom Act, which gives legal rights to Native Peoples to their traditional ceremonies and rituals, sacred sites and public lands for ceremonial purposes, and the use of their religious symbols (feathers, tobacco, sweet grass,

bones, etc.) for use in their traditional ceremonies and rituals.[75]

One more example is the Indian Arts and Crafts Act of 1990. Though the Indian Arts and Crafts Board was created by the Act of August 27, 1935, which

> was responsible for promoting and developing of American Indian and Alaska Native arts and crafts, improving the economic status of members of Federally-recognized tribes [by the way, there are still quite many tribes that are not Federally-recognized — O.D.], and helping to develop and expand marketing opportunities for arts and crafts produced by American Indians and Alaska Natives,[76]

it was not observed carefully enough. In response to growing sales in the billion dollars U.S. American Indian arts and crafts market of products misrepresented or erroneously represented as produced by American Indians, the Congress passed the Act of 1990. It is "essentially a truth-in-advertising law designed to prevent marketing products as "Indian made"

---

[75] Ryan, J.B. Listening to Native Americans // Listening: Journal of Religion and Culture, Vol. 31, No.1 Winter 1996 pp. 24-36, [online] Available at: <http://www.op.org/DomCentral/library/native.htm> [Accessed 06 March 2002].
[76] Ibid.

when the products are not, in fact, made by Indians as defined by the Act."[77] Thus, ancient traditions can continue, but the degree of harm that was done to them is unmeasurable – some traditions became extinct, many of them are on the verge of extinction...

And still, despite all the difficulties,

> the historical destinies of individual American Indian cultures, as well as their entirety in the United States, have demonstrated a lesson in spiritual survival and ability to adapt to an unfavorable environment, first natural, then more socio-cultural. Moreover, they found an amazing ability to incorporate alien elements into their culture without losing their own identity[78],

thus giving an example to other indigenous peoples.

---

[77] Ibid.
[78] Ващенко, А.В. Культура, мифология и фольклор американских индейцев доколониальной эпохи. // История литературы США. Т.1. М.: Наследие, 1997. С. 39-88. С. 86.

Chapter 4. The Analysis of *House Made of Dawn* and *Ceremony*

4.1. N. Scott Momaday and Leslie Marmon Silko

Navarre Scott Momaday is a special figure even inside American Indian literature. He was born in 1934 in Oklahoma and grew up on the Navajo reservation. Since his childhood both by his origin (his father had the blood of a Kiowa and his mother — of the English and Cherokee) and by his upbringing he has been a representative of two worlds — the world of American Indians (mainly Kiowa) and the world of white Americans. N. Scott Momaday is at the same time a novelist, poet, playwright, painter, teacher of American Indian literature, and a public figure dedicated to the preservation of Native American culture. He has always been interested in the traditions, customs and beliefs of American Indians, many of which are easily recognizable in his works (for example, the play *Children of the Sun* based on the material of the mythology of his native tribe, the narrative-ritual *The Way to Rainy Mountain* as a "book about culture", two series of American Indian shields combining elements of fine and literary art, etc.). His most famous novel, which began American Indian Renaissance, is *House*

Made of Dawn written in 1968. The novel immediately gained fame and was soon translated into German, French, Polish and Russian, and in 1969 the author was awarded the Pulitzer Prize for it. For an invaluable contribution to literature, in 1997 the writer was presented to the Nobel Prize. And yet the most important thing, in our opinion, is that N. Scott Momaday is the pioneer of the literature of Native Americans (*House Made of Dawn* is considered the first sample of ethnic literature in America). Among his other famous works is the novel *Ancient Child*, a collection of articles and essays *The Man Made of Words*, two books on American Indian culture — *The Native Americans: Indian County* and *Circle of Wonder: A Native American Christmas History*, *In the Bear's House*, and others.

N. Scott Momaday has always been focused on Kiowa traditions, customs and beliefs, and is also recognized as one of the most successful contemporary Native American literary figures.

Leslie Marmon Silko, the first American Indian woman-writer, is also of mixed origin: Mexican, white and Laguna Pueblo. She was born in 1948 in Albuquerque, New Mexico, and grew up on the Laguna Pueblo reservation — a place that, as she said, had a huge impact on her as a person and writer. In the development of the "story-telling" and literary life of L.M. Silko a very important role was played by her great-grandmother (she was for the author the same inexhaustible source of traditions and stories of her people as N. Scott Momaday's grandmother for him). L.M. Silko saw her goal in the use of her own narrative talent in support of the cultural survival of her people. She tried to combine the old and new rituals and ceremonies of the Laguna Pueblo to adapt them to modern life on reservations, and sought to show that traditional stories still live. She is a novelist, a poet (in 1974 she was awarded a prize for poetry), a folklorist and a teacher. Of particular interest, in our opinion, is her novel *Ceremony* published in 1977, the main milestone in her work. In this novel, mythology and the plot are so intertwined that it is not possible to separate them. No less famous is her novel *Almanac of the Dead*. Among her other works we should mention *Gardens in the Dunes*, a collection of autobiographical stories *Storyteller*, as well as collections of poems.

Both authors have their origins in American Indian tribes. That permits them to write from within, knowing all the traditions and customs of Native Americans, their life and inner world. We realize that to say "to know someone's inner world" means to understand the deepest movements and desires of his soul, but in this case we are strongly convinced that one may speak about some generalized American Indian soul with no respect to a person's tribal origin, age or sex. Further on we would try to prove this idea through the usage of Native American mythology and the role of words in the studied books. Hence, we agree to use the terms "American Indian", "an American Indian soul" or "an American Indian's inner world" relating to any man or woman of American Indian ancestry. Other terms that we would like to allot are "white world" and "white man". We use these terms in our book, as well as they are used in many critical works, as an opposition to "American Indian world" and "an American Indian" only, without any shade of evaluation to either of them. For stylistic purposes, the terms "American Indian" and "Native American" are used interchangeably.

The novels *House of the Dawn* by N. Scott Momaday and *Ceremony* by L.M. Silko have much in common: starting with the American Indian origin of the authors, the ideas, the region described, the myths and mythological plots used, and endings and the destinies of the protagonists. But the main thing, to our mind, is the commonality of the themes and ideas. In both works, the theme of man's spiritual development through self-awareness and his place in life and the idea of a clash of two worlds and cultures (of Native Americans and Euro-Americans) are very well represented. The protagonists face a choice between these two worlds, and, what is especially important from the point of view of culture, make it in favor of the Native American one. Both writers conduct their protagonists through the thorny path of moral and physical trials and temptations, put them in situations that obstruct making the final choice. But, with the help of American Indian friends, medicine men, visions, etc. to the heroes' help comes the ancient wisdom of American Indian people, which leads them to realize the vital role of traditions and returns them to their tribe, where they find a lost harmony with the surrounding world and with themselves.

A significant similarity is observed in the plots as well.

House Made of Dawn. A prologue describes a young man running into the dawn. The story proper begins when Abel returns to his Pueblo, Walatowa (Jemez) at the end of his wartime service. He tries to fit back into the Pueblo way of life, but is unable to make a smooth transition, partly because he was not at peace with himself when he left, and partly due to his collision with the world of the whites not from its most pleasant side. Abel's mother died when he was small as did his brother Vidal. He was raised by his grandfather, Francisco, the son of a priest who served at the Pueblo in the 1870s. Abel meets a pregnant woman, Angela St. John, and has a brief alliance with her. Several days after the Feast of Santiago, where an albino man wins the "rooster pull" and flails Abel with the dead rooster, apparently as part of the game, Abel kills "the white man" outside a bar where they both had been drinking. The next section of the novel takes place in Los Angeles in 1952 on the night that Abel receives a horrible beating. As Abel drifts in and out of consciousness, we learn about the past six years of his life, his time in prison, his relocation to California, his affair with a social worker named Milly, and his friendship with Benally, a Navajo. Superimposed on Abel's delirious state is the sermon and peyote ceremony led by J.B.B. Tosamah, Priest of the Sun. In these ceremonies, the only way of salvation for those like him is shown, which is returning to traditions. The third part of the book takes place a month later and is told by Benally who provides even more information about Abel's uneasy relocation to Los Angeles. While Abel was in hospital, Angela came to visit him. In this part of the novel Benally performs a Navajo chant aimed at healing the friend. Benally says that Abel and him had plans to go back home together. In the last part of the novel Abel goes home to Walatowa in February and watches over the death bed of his grandfather. Each morning for six days the old man wakes and speaks. On the seventh morning he dies. Abel performs the appropriate ceremony for his grandfather and then, having realized that he is part of American Indian world, goes out to participate in the traditional dawn race with the sun, which are held to maintain the cyclicality and eternity of being. He is finally healed and has found his place in life, having returned to his native tribe.

Ceremony. Tayo, a mixed-blood character (half-Indian, half-white) who was raised in his aunt's house, returns to his Pueblo from World War II mentally and physically ill. His cousin, Rocky, was killed in the war and Josiah, his uncle, died while he was away. Tayo feels responsible for both deaths. He spends a lot of time drinking with his buddies and telling war stories. One war buddy, Emo, is particularly twisted, and he and Tayo had a run-in soon after they returned. An old medicine man, Ku'oosh, treats Tayo, but suspects that there is more wrong than he can cure. Tayo offers to begin helping out his Uncle Robert with the ranch work and they plan to get back the spotted cattle that were stolen from Josiah during the war. Robert takes him to Gallup where he meets Betonie, a mixed-blood medicine man. Betonie makes a sand painting and tells Tayo he must find a woman, a mountain, the cattle, and the pattern of stars in the painting to complete the ceremony. When Tayo goes up the mountain to round up the stolen cattle, he sees the star pattern in the sky. He discovers that a woman has corralled the cattle for him. Later on, when Tayo returns to the ranch, he finds the woman has already set up camp there. They spend the summer together, she collecting plants, he tending the cattle. Finally, Robert arrives and tells Tayo that Emo has started rumors about him, that it is time to go back home. On the way home, Tayo is met on the road by his friends Leroy and Harley. Thinking that the "witchery" must not extend to friends, he goes with them, getting so drunk he passes out. When he wakes, he realizes he is in danger, and begins to run with the sun. He rests at an abandoned uranium mine and recognizes that everything is connected: the uranium from this mine went into the bomb that killed the Japanese that killed Rocky. Fearful of discovery, Tayo hides in a culvert. His friends arrive and Emo proceeds to torture Harley gruesomely. Tayo uses all his newfound understanding to resist the impulse to participate in the hatred by killing Emo. He heads for home, crossing the river at sunrise on the day of the autumn equinox. Tayo tells his story to the men in the kiva[79]. Harley and Leroy are found dead in the wrecked truck. Pinkie is killed by Emo, who is banished. Grandma comments that she thinks she's heard these stories before. The witchery is "dead for now," and the sun rises, greeted by a prayer.

---

[79] Kiva — a round-shaped traditional construction of the Pueblo Indians used for ceremonial purposes and political meetings.

4.2. The Use of American Indian Mythology in the Novels

The compositions of both novels, though not identical, on the whole are quite similar. In both books there is a cyclicality, although in *House Made of Dawn* this is expressed most clearly.

The prologue of N. Scott Momaday's novel speaks about the same situation as the end of the book: Abel's running in the Winter Race at the dawn, but if in the beginning "he seemed almost to be standing still"[80], in the end "all of his being was concentrated in the sheer motion of running on."[81] This stylistic method underlines the idea of the change that happened in Abel's soul even more, it makes this change almost vivid: from a "cul-de-sac" with stillness and inner indifference to motion and emotions.

The first and the last words of the novel, "*dypaloh*" and "*qtsedaba*", announce that the story being framed in a specifically Towan or Jemez story, while the first and last sentences of the story so framed ("There was a house made of dawn"; "*House made of pollen, house made of*

---

[80] Momaday, N.S. House Made of Dawn. N.Y.: Signet, 1969. P. 7.
[81] Ibid., p. 191.

dawn") paraphrase the opening lines of a traditional Navajo chant.[82]

Ceremony opens with three original stories (it should also be indicated that the majority if not all Native American stories used in this book are presented in a poem-like form with blank verse, which is used by the author when she created her own stories, too): the creation myth describing the creation of the world by one of the most important figures in Pueblo mythology – Thought Woman, then a passage emphasizing the important role that storytelling plays within the Pueblo culture, and finally a short passage representing the words about the importance of ceremonies in Pueblo medicine. But the first word of the novel itself is "sunrise". The novel finishes with the story of the witchery which "is dead for now" and a three-line passage after it:

Sunrise,
accept this offering,
Sunrise.

The words make the accents in the book: they show that everything in the world is connected with nature's ways and, like the sun, the protagonist "rises" after his illness again. Here the most powerful figure of Pueblo mythology is

---

[82] Nelson, R.M. Place and Vision. The Function of Landscape in Native American Fiction. 1999, [online] Available at: <http://www.richmond.edu/~rnelson/PandV/front.html> [Accessed 25 December 2001].

"patronizing" Tayo – Sun Father. Thus, the novel has poem-like stories and the same word which figure in the beginning as well as in the end. Though there are other poems met in the narration (and they are present in both books), the poem "Ceremony" parallels the novel: this story is told in parts in different places of the text and helps L.M. Silko connect the ceremony of Tayo's curing with old traditions and show once again the importance of a ceremony.

Both *House Made of Dawn* and *Ceremony* begin and end with a sunrise, show the spiritual development of the main characters through Native American mythology, convince that man should never forget his traditions, and emphasize the creative power of the word. And one more interesting thing: the most important story in *Ceremony* has the same title as the title of the book, and the same situation is with *House Made of Dawn* and its principal chant. So, a conclusion may be drawn that N.S. Momaday and L.M. Silko used such stylistic devices as similar beginning and end reinforced by traditional American Indian poems and the titles of their books same as the names of the poems to create a special atmosphere in their narration, to show the moral development of their protagonists and to prove their point of view that a person should never forget his traditions.

As mentioned above, these novels are of particular value from the point of view of culture due to the organic use of myths and mythological plots in them, which requires special attention.

4.3. *House Made of Dawn*

The main poem of the novel is the prayer "House Made of Dawn" which paraphrases the contents metaphorically and leads back to old traditions, as well as gives the novel its title. This healing Night Chant performed by Abel's friend, Benally, is Navajo in origin. Besides its beauty, it has a great power and is supposed to help Abel to heal him, and is sung only to be heard by two people – the protagonist and the singer not to interfere with its holiness: "I started to sing all by myself. The others were singing, too, but it was the wrong kind of thing, and I wanted to pray. I didn't want them to hear me, because they were having a good time, and I was ashamed, I guess. I kept it down because I didn't want anybody but him to hear."[83]

> House made of dawn,
> House made of evening light,
> House made of dark cloud,
> House made of male rain,
> House made of dark mist,
> House made of female rain,
> House made of pollen,
> House made of grasshoppers,
> Dark cloud is at the door.

---
[83] Momaday, N.S. House Made of Dawn. N.Y.: Signet, 1969. P. 133-4.

The trail out of it is dark cloud.
The zigzag lightning stands high upon it.
Male deity!
Your offering I make.
I have prepared a smoke for you.
Restore my feet for me,
Restore my legs for me,
Restore my body for me,
Restore my mind for me,
Restore my voice for me.
This very day take out your spell for me.
Your spell remove from me.
You have taken it away for me;
Far off it has gone.
Happily I recover.
Happily my interior becomes cool.
Happily I go forth.
My interior feeling cool, may I walk.
No longer sore, may I walk.
Impervious to pain, may I walk.
With lively feelings, may I walk.
As it used to be long ago, may I walk.
Happily may I walk.
Happily, with abundant dark clouds, may I walk.
Happily, with abundant showers, may I walk.
Happily, with abundant plants, may I walk.

> Happily, on a trail of pollen, may I walk.
> Happily may I walk.
> Being as it used to be long ago, may I walk.
> May it be beautiful before me,
> May it be beautiful behind me,
> May it be beautiful below me,
> May it be beautiful above me,
> May it be beautiful all around me.
> In beauty it is finished.[84]

The performing of this chant may be called one of the most important moments in the book, maybe even one of its climaxes (we say "one of" because the main one goes further). N.S. Momaday managed to express Abel's state of soul and position, Benally's attitude to him and desire to help, the importance of traditions and the belief in the healing power of the word in one very song which combined everything. This stylistic device returns the reader to the first and sends him later to the last sentences of the novel, thus uniting the beginning, the development and the end of Abel's story.

The other prayer appears in the same part of the book, "The Night Chanter", when "the act of imagining Abel's return to the land recalls to

---

[84] Momaday, N.S. House Made of Dawn. N.Y.: Signet, 1969. P. 134-5.

Ben his own experience of returning to the land after having been away from it for a few years"[85], and while imagining himself returning home "like a man, on a black and beautiful horse"[86], he remembers that "it was good going out like that, and it made you want to pray."[87] The prayer of a rider proud of his horse, full of beautiful metaphors and comparisons, follows his recollections:

> I am the Turquoise Woman's son.[88]
> On top of Belted Mountain,
> Beautiful horse – slim like a weasel.
> My horse has a hoof like striped agate;

---

[85] Nelson, R.M. Place and Vision. The Function of Landscape in Native American Fiction. 1999, [online] Available at: <http://www.richmond.edu/~rnelson/PandV/front.html> [Accessed 25 December 2001]. Ch. 2.

[86] Momaday, N.S. House Made of Dawn. N.Y.: Signet, 1969. P. 154.

[87] Ibid., p. 155.

[88] Turquoise Woman, or Changing Woman (Navajo name — Estsanatlehi) is the Navajo's female head goddess. She is the Sky Goddess who "became the Sun's wife and had two twins from him — Monster Slayer and Born for Water, who later became culture heroes. She is the symbol of creation, protection and prolificacy, the ancestor of six first Navajo clans and a number of sacred ceremonies (initiation ceremony for girls and Beauty Way) which are still held, and is an example for all mothers". (Danchevskaya, O.Y. Turquoise in the Life of American Indians. Images, Imaginations, and Beyond. Proceedings of the Eighth Native American Symposium. Ed. by Mark B. Spencer. Durant, Oklahoma: Southeastern Oklahoma State University, 2010. P. 144-149. P. 146. (Also available online at: <http://homepages.se.edu/nas/files/2013/03/NAS-2009-Proceedings-Danchevskaya.pdf>))

His fetlock is like a fine eagle plume;
His legs are like quick lightning.
My horse's body is like an eagle-plumed arrow;
My horse has a tail like a trailing black cloud.
I put flexible goods on my horse's back;
The Little Holy Wind blows through his hair.
His mane is made of short rainbows.
My horse's ears are made of round corn.
My horse's eyes are made of big stars.
My horse's head is made of mixed waters –
From the holy waters – he never knows thirst.
My horse's teeth are made of white shell.
The long rainbow is in his mouth for a bridle,
and with it I guide him.
When my horse neighs, different-colored horses
follow.
When my horse neighs, different-colored sheep
follow.
I am wealthy, because of him.
Before me peaceful,

> Behind me peaceful,
> Under me peaceful,
> Over me peaceful,
> All around me peaceful –
> Peaceful voice when he neighs.
> I am Everlasting and Peaceful.
> I stand for my horse.[89]

This prayer, this song helps the reader understand two things: the crucial role of the word in an American Indian perception of the world and Benally's personality and the desire of his unspoiled soul to pray when he sees beauty or wants to help someone. Again, as with the previous song, Momaday found the best possible way to express feelings in words.

The book also contains stories in prose. There are three of them, two in the part called *The Priest of the Sun* and one in *The Night Chanter*, each conveying a special stylistic purpose. The first one, the story of "how Tai-me came to the Kiowas" ("the Kiowas were a sun dance culture, and Tai-me was their sun dance doll, their most sacred fetish; no medicine was ever more powerful")[90], is told by Tosamah, the Priest of the Sun, during his sermon at the place

---

[89] Momaday, N.S. House Made of Dawn. N.Y.: Signet, 1969. P. 155.
[90] Ibid., p. 89.

where he speaks about "the Word" and the different attitudes to it by "the white man's world" and American Indians. As an example he takes his grandmother for whom stories were holy, and this story is one of them. Right after it Tosamah explains its meaning: "The story of the coming of Tai-me has existed for hundreds of years by word of mouth. It represents the oldest idea that a man has of himself."[91] This story interlaces perfectly with the whole sermon and strengthens the contrast between white men's attitude to the word and that of American Indians. It parallels the Christian version of creation ("In the beginning was the Word...") taken as the basis for this sermon, but from a Native American angle: "Far, far away in the nothingness something happened. There was a voice, a sound, a word – and everything began."[92] It describes how American Indians got the Word and thus explains their special respect for it. "Why are you following me? What do you want?" And from that day the Word has belonged to us, who have heard it for what it is, who have lived in fear and awe of it."[93] With the help of this story N. Scott Momaday not only did give a good example of American Indian folklore preserved by storytellers, but also

---

[91] Ibid.
[92] Ibid., p. 90.
[93] Ibid., p. 91.

supported the ideas preached by the Priest of the Sun and showed how easy it is to find harmony, while white people may write piles of books only to describe it.

Then there goes only a short summary of the Kiowa creation myth given again by Tosamah as he heard it from his grandmother being a child: "According to their creation myth, they entered the world through a hollow log. From one point of view, their migration was the fruit of an old prophecy, for indeed they emerged from a sunless world."[94] The introductory constructions in this quote show the influence of living surrounded by the white culture (in Los Angeles) and getting the whites' education.

Just a couple of paragraphs further appears the second story. Following the ancient way of migration of his people, Tosamah found himself once in a beautiful place in the hills.

> There are things in nature which engender an awful quiet in the heart of man; Devils Tower is one of them. Many must account for it. He must never fail to explain such a thing to himself, or else he is estranged forever from the universe. Two centuries

---

[94] Momaday, N.S. House Made of Dawn. N.Y.: Signet, 1969. P. 119.

ago, because they could not do otherwise, the Kiowas made a legend at the base of the rock[95], and he tells this "story of how Devils Tower[96] was created when six sisters climbed to the top of a tree that grew to the sky to escape their brother who had become a bear. They became the stars of the Big Dipper."[97] Later on Abel remembers this story, and this recollection serves as a reminder that he has "kinsmen in the night sky"[98] – another helpful straw for him, "a way out of the wilderness."[99] This story demonstrates American Indian worldview – the fact that all is alive and interdependent. With its help Tosamah describes the magical spell that nature (and not only Devils Tower) has over a person.

The last story in the book is presented absolutely differently. When Angela, the white woman with whom Abel had an affair several

---

[95] Ibid., p. 120.
[96] Devils Tower — an unusual looking butte in the Bear Lodge Mountains (part of the Black Hills). It is mentioned in the myths of several Native American tribes (the Kiowa, the Lakota, the Sioux, the Cheyenne among them).
[97] Мелетинский, Е.М. (ред.) Мифологический словарь. М.: Советская энциклопедия, 1991.
[98] Momaday, N.S. House Made of Dawn. N.Y.: Signet, 1969. P. 121.
[99] Ibid.

years before, comes to see him in the hospital, she

> started telling him about her son, Peter. ...Peter always asked her about the Indians, she said, and she used to tell him a story about a young Indian brave. He was born of a bear and a maiden, she said, and he was noble and wise. He had many adventures, and he became a great leader and saved his people. It was the story Peter liked best of all, and she always thought of *him*, Abel, when she told it.[100]

But as all this is only Benally's recollections of the past, he continues the narration and mocks a little at Angela: "Ei yei! A bear! A bear and a maiden. And she was a white woman and she thought it up, you know, made it up out of her own mind, and it was like that old grandfather talking to me, telling me about *Esdzá shash nadle*, or *Dzil quigi*, yes, just like that"[101], and tells the story as he heard it from his grandfather who "knew everything and there was no end to the stories and the songs."[102] At this moment the reader realizes that not only American Indians are influenced by white people, but sometimes vice

---

[100] Momaday, N.S. House Made of Dawn. N.Y.: Signet, 1969. P. 169.
[101] Ibid., p. 170.
[102] Ibid.

versa as well, and then American Indian folklore serves a different purpose – it educates a person and gives him a basic knowledge of how American Indians view the world and of their culture and history. By this story N.S. Momaday showed Angela's attitude to Abel, something more intimate than simple words may say, and her prone (what was already felt from the very beginning of the book) more to American Indian than to white perception of life, which developed and was passed on to her son (the way Native Americans do, from generation to generation). Thus, the main reason to use American Indian stories *in House Made of Dawn* may be that of justifying of the words, feelings and actions of people and showing the interrelation of everything in the universe.

4.4. *Ceremony*

The analysis of *Ceremony* was held against the same criteria, and the following results were received. L.M. Silko's use of stories is rather different from N. Scott Momaday's. The first distinction is in their form: if in in *House Made of Dawn* there are only two poems, and even they are not quite stories but prayers; others are either presented in a prose form or are mixed with the narration and are part of the text, in *Ceremony* mostly poems are met (all the stories except "Note on Bear People and Witches" and Tayo's story in the kiva). Like in Momaday's book, there is the leading story in Silko's novel as well – this is "Ceremony", which also gives the novel its title (similar to Momaday's "House Made of Dawn").

In the novel, there are about thirty poems based on Native American mythology, and they all are different. Some of them are separated and told in parts what makes a specific background to the main text (like "Ceremony" or the story of the child taken by bears), others are whole; old traditional stories (as the one about the coming of white people) neighbour with the contemporary ones about present life (the war veteran's story); some of them are only several lines (as some parts of "Ceremony"), others are relatively long (as the story about Ch'o'yo's magic). But the main question for us is not to compare them but to see how and why the writer used them and indicate especially important places. For this purpose we suggest studying the poems from the very beginning of the book.

The first poem in the text is about Reed Woman and her sister Corn Woman who
>... got angry
>and scolded
>her sister
>for bathing all day long[103],

and she went away.
>And there was no more rain then.
>Everything dried up
>all the plants
>the corn
>the beans
>they all dried up
>and started blowing away
>in the wind.[104]

This poem is introduced right in the place where Tayo thinks about the drought and remembers that once he "prayed the rain away"[105],

---

[103] Silko, L.M. Ceremony. N.Y.: Signet, 1978. P. 13.
[104] Ibid.
[105] Ibid., p. 13.

showing the close connection between a person and nature typical of American Indian psychology. The following poem is about "Scalp Society" and it proves the words of the old medicine man Ku'oosh about the whites that "not even oldtime witches killed like that."[106] The next story supports the words of Tayo's uncle Josiah: "The old people used to say that droughts happen when people forget, when people misbehave"[107] and describes how people, even the twin brothers Ma'see'wi and Ou'yo'ye'wi, the traditional mythological heroes, "were fooled by ... Ch'o'yo medicine man, Pa'caya'nyi" and his magic, and thus neglected "our mother Nau'ts'ityi",

        So she took
the plants and grass from them.
No baby animals were born.
        She took the
        rainclouds with her.[108]

This story stresses once more how important it is to be in harmony with nature for an American Indian. Further on this story – which is the main of all the poems in the book – is continued: it describes how people noticed a hummingbird (a typical mythological figure in Pueblo mythology) who "was fat and shiny"[109],

---

[106] Silko, L.M. Ceremony. N.Y.: Signet, 1978. P. 13.
[107] Ibid., p. 47.
[108] Ibid., p. 50.

then asked him for help, and he said they needed a messenger and explained how to prepare a ceremonial jar[110]; how

       ... a big green fly
    with yellow feelers on his head
       flew out of the jar[111]

on the fourth day, the fly who was the messenger, and they both flew to Corn Mother; how they found her and

   ... gave her blue pollen and yellow pollen
    they gave her turquoise beads[112]
    they gave her prayer sticks[113]

and she said they needed "old Buzzard to purify" their town first; how they "went to see old Buzzard" and he said about their pollen, beads and prayer sticks that their offering wasn't complete without the tobacco[114]; how Fly and Hummingbird had to return to the people and then to the mother because the former had no

---

[109] Ibid., p. 56.
[110] Ibid., p. 74.
[111] Ibid., p. 86.
[112] Turquoise is the most beloved semi-precious stone of Native Americans. For more information, see: Danchevskaya, O.Y. Turquoise in the Life of American Indians. Images, Imaginations, and Beyond. Proceedings of the Eighth Native American Symposium. Ed. by Mark B. Spencer. Durant, Oklahoma: Southeastern Oklahoma State University, 2010. P. 144-149. P. 146. (Also available online at: <http://homepages.se.edu/nas/files/2013/03/NAS-2009-Proceedings-Danchevskaya.pdf>)
[113] Silko, L.M. Ceremony. N.Y.: Signet, 1978. P. 110.
[114] Ibid., p. 119.

tobacco[115]; how Caterpillar gave them tobacco[116]; and finally how old Buzzard accepted the offering and purified the town and
> The storm clouds returned
> the grass and plants started growing again.
> There was food
> and the people were happy again.[117]

But there was a warning from their mother:
> Stay out of trouble
> from now on.
> It isn't very easy
> to fix up things again.[118]

This poem parallels the novel, and each new part of this longest and very rich in detail from American Indian mythology poem marks a new step in the ceremony of healing Tayo and illustrates how easy it is to get into trouble and how difficult it is to get out of it. In the end, when the ceremony is successfully finished and the protagonist is cured, rain clouds (the symbol of fertility) and felicity return to the people. L.M. Silko used a very efficient stylistic device to speak about an American Indian ceremony and the way of life; without the poem the novel would have lost a great part of its charm and original power.

---

[115] Silko, L.M. Ceremony. N.Y.: Signet, 1978. P. 159.
[116] Ibid., p. 187-8.
[117] Ibid., p. 268.
[118] Ibid.

There are also several other stories-poems in the book, and they bear an important stylistic function as well. One of them starts when Tayo is found in the old medicine man's place and is introduced to his helper Shush, which means "bear"; Tayo noticed that "there was something strange about the boy, something remote in his eyes, as if he were on a distant mountaintop alone and the fire and the hogan[119] and the lights of the town below them did not exist."[120] Then we read this story about the child who went to a bear's cave and though was taken back later by medicine men,

> ... he wasn't quite the same
> after that
> not like the other children.[121]

In this place a metaphor may be clearly seen and it is possible to transform the myth, where a bear's cave would represent white people and the period Tayo was at war, medicine men – those who tried to cure him, and the child – the protagonist himself. But then follows a very important passage – "Note on Bear People and Witches" where the two of them are differentiated, bear people living with bears and

---

[119] Hogan — a traditional Navajo dwelling.
[120] Silko, L.M. Ceremony. N.Y.: Signet, 1978. P. 135.
[121] Ibid., p. 137.

not being "conscious of being different from their bear relatives", and witches being able to "do nothing but play around with objects and bodies" and of whom animals are terrified because "they smell the death".[122] It proves that Tayo can be regarded as a "bear person", not as a "witch", that is being influenced from outside but remaining innocent and pure inside, which gives much more chances that the treatment will be successful.

Later we find a story about a young man who was turned into a coyote and how his relatives went to the old Bear People for help, and it is told at the moment when a similar ritual is going to be held over Tayo by the new medicine man, Betonie, who makes drawings and preparations very similar to the ones mentioned in the poem. Then there is the continuation to the story describing the ceremony of the curing of the young man which is interrupted by the very ceremony of curing Tayo. Both ceremonies are finished at the same time, but in the poem the last lines say:

>and he recovered
>he stood up
>The rainbows returned him to his
>   home, but it wasn't over.

---

[122] Silko, L.M. Ceremony. N.Y.: Signet, 1978. P. 137.

> All kinds of evil were still on him.[123]

It leads the reader to believe that it is not the end yet. Again, L.M. Silko used the same method to strengthen the tension of the description of the ceremony and its role, and this comparison – which we dare call a metaphor with some features of a parallel construction – is another example of the complexity and originality of the book. A number of pages further it is discovered that the hint given by that poem is true, and "the ceremony isn't finished yet"[124], what is supported by the next poem (which continues the previous one by the meaning but has a bit different form):

> The dry skin
> was still stuck
> to his body.[125]

These were the main stories backing up the text, but there are some minor ones which are also very interesting.

Besides the stories, there are two songs which also have a stylistic purpose. One of them has the first and the last words of the novel in it, "sunrise":

> Sunrise!

---

[123] Ibid., p 151.
[124] Ibid., p. 160.
[125] Ibid.

> We come at sunrise
> to greet you.
> We call you
> at sunrise.
> Father of the clouds
> you are beautiful
> at sunrise.
> Sunrise![126]

This song is recollected by Tayo at the dawn, when he travels alone in search of the spotted cattle and keeps repeating one word – "sunrise". Thus, a traditional dawn song becomes a prayer, a symbol of purification and the reunity with Mother Earth. The protagonist "wakes up" after his "night" – illness as the sun rises every morning, and nothing can change this movement.

The other song is sung by a hunter whom Tayo meets: "Then behind him he heard someone singing. A man singing a chant. He stopped and listened. His stomach froze tight, and sweat ran down his ribs. His heart was pounding, but he was more startled than afraid."[127] "He recognized phrases of the song; he had heard the hunters sing it, late in October, while they waited for the deer to be driven down from the high slopes by the cold winds and the snow."[128] That hunter

---

[126] Silko, L.M. Ceremony. N.Y.: Signet, 1978. P. 189-190.
[127] Ibid., p. 215.

looks very traditional and his game – a deer – is decorated with "delicate blue feathers"[129], according to the ritual that all hunters are supposed to perform. All this is one more step on Tayo's way back to his tribe, and the song draws some link to the old style of life.

Probably the most interesting is the story of Emo, one of Tayo's friends before World War II, which shows the impact of the war on American Indians and the way it destroyed them both mentally and physically.

> Rather than giving the men a new life, World War II destroys them. Rocky is killed fighting the Japanese, Emo becomes an alcoholic, and Tayo returns with a severe case of post-traumatic stress disorder that white medicine has been unable to cure. In his search for healing, Tayo first turns to drinking with Emo and the other American Indian veterans. But becoming part of a pattern of drinking and violence never before witnessed among American Indian veterans only makes Tayo sicker. Rather than telling traditional stories about the people's relationship with the earth and the deities, the American Indian veterans tell

---

[128] Ibid., p. 216.
[129] Ibid., p. 217.

stories about the witchery of the modern world, which has tricked them into believing it is good, just as the Ch'o'yo magician tricked the Pueblos into believing his magic was enough to sustain life. The distortion the witchery has produced in ritual storytelling can be seen in the following myth which Emo tells[130]:

We went into this bar on 4th Ave., see,
  me and O'Shay, this crazy Irishman.
    We had a few drinks, then I saw
        these two white women
          sitting all alone.
        One was kind of fat
         She had dark hair.
      But this other one, man,
        she had big tits and
          real blond hair.
           I said to him
   "Hey buddy, that's the one I want.
            Over there."
    He said, "Go get'em, Chief."
  He was my best drinking buddy, that guy
          He'd watch me
  see how good I'd score with each one.[131]

---

[130] Austgen, S.M. Leslie Marmon Silko's Ceremony and the Effect of White Contact on Pueblo Myth and Ritual, [online] Available at:
<http://history.hanover.edu/hhr/hhr93_2.html> [Accessed 14 January 2007].

Here L.M. Silko uses a modern story to show the real influence of the war, which is compared by American Indians themselves with a "witchery", and another story continues these sad contemplations – about the witchery that made white people appear and gave arms to them. This story is very typical of the American Indian view of the world and so traditional on the one hand, but so full of despair on the other, that it unites all that can be said in the novel about the whites and their life. There was a gathering of witches "from all directions ... and all tribes"[132], and there was a contest between them. Only one witch did not show off , and

> no one ever knew where this witch came from
> which tribe
> or if it was a woman or a man[133],

but this witch tells them: "What I have is a story"[134], and it is about how she created white people, and as she tells the story "it will begin to happen."[135] Some lines strike anybody's imagination, like these ones:

> The world is a dead thing for them
> the trees and rivers are not alive

---

[131] Silko, L.M. Ceremony. N.Y.: Signet, 1978. P. 59-60.
[132] Ibid., p. 140.
[133] Ibid., p. 141.
[134] Ibid.
[135] Ibid.

the mountains and stones are not alive.
The deer and bear are objects
They see no life.
They fear
They fear the world.
They destroy what they fear.
They fear themselves.
The wind will blow them across the ocean
thousands of them in giant boats
swarming like larva
out of crushed and hill.
They will carry objects
which can shoot death
faster than the eye can see.
They will kill the things they fear
all the animals
the people will starve.
They will poison the water
they will spin the water away
and there will be drought
the people will starve.
They will fear what they find
They will fear the people
They kill what they fear.
Entire villages will be wiped out
They will slaughter whole tribes.
Corpses for us
Blood for us
Killing killing killing killing.

And those they do not kill
will die anyway
at the destruction they see
at the loss
at the loss of the children
the loss will destroy the rest.
Stolen rivers and mountains
the stolen land will eat their hearts
and jerk their mouths from the Mother.
The people will starve.
They will bring terrible diseases
the people have never known.
Entire tribes will die out
covered with festered sores
shitting blood
vomiting blood.
Corpses for our work
set in motion now
set in motion by our witchery
set in motion
to work for us.[136]

And when the others ask the witch to "call that story back"[137], they get the answer:

It's already turned loose.
It's already coming.
It can't be called back.[138]

---

[136] Silko, L.M. Ceremony. N.Y.: Signet, 1978. P. 143-4.
[137] Ibid., p. 145.
[138] Ibid.

All this is the story old Betonie tells Tayo to explain that it were American Indians who made white people appear, only with the help of a story[139], and to say that they "can deal with [them] …, with their machines and beliefs."[140] But this witchery turns out to be a disaster for an American Indian world, and though the teller tries to soften its consequences, we cannot but feel how grave it is, and Leslie Marmon Silko helps us realize it. With this story we may understand the reasons for a specific attitude to the whites and their world from American Indians, and this poem may be regarded as one of the most efficient stylistic devices of the author. Were it just a paraphrasing of the traditional story, it would lose its power, but its originality goes straight to the heart, and though one may argue about its reliability, one cannon help feeling that it bears a lot of truth about present-day life and about the past ("shitting blood vomiting blood" – this is the description of smallpox brought by the Spanish invaders). Thus, the creation story of white people is very important for the book; it draws a traditional boundary between American Indians and the white world.

---

[139] On the power of word, see Part 1.2.
[140] Silko, L.M. Ceremony. N.Y.: Signet, 1978. P. 139.

At the end of the book the writer gives a different story – the one Tayo tells old Ku'oosh and other Pueblo elders in the kiva of the "genetrix spirit he has encountered in the land..."[141] This story crowns the narration; it may be treated as the climax of the novel, and if the stories told before were mostly traditional (except Emo's one), this one is told by the protagonist himself and is about his own experience. This is not a narration inside a narration, but the main text, and once more it shows the importance of storytelling and of the connection with the Earth for Native Americans. This story has also other functions. According to R.M. Nelson, part of the appeal of Tayo's story to the kiva elders is that it reestablishes the Pueblo as the geographical (and hence spiritual) center of a visible world, a particular landscape that contains, within itself, the power to heal and make whole and sustain life in the face of those destructive forces (both internal and external to human consciousness) that cohabit the universe.[142]

---

[141] Nelson, R.M. Place and Vision. The Function of Landscape in Native American Fiction. 1999, [online] Available at: <http://www.richmond.edu/~rnelson/PandV/front.html> [Accessed 25 December 2001]. Ch. 1.
[142] Ibid.

4.5. Comparison of *House Made of Dawn* and *Ceremony*

In the previous chapters the stories and songs used in the novels *House Made of Dawn* and *Ceremony* were studied. There are some other features that are worthwhile to comment on regarding the "Native American trace" in these books. As the analysis has shown, Leslie Marmon Silko used Pueblo myths (except the veteran's story), while N. Scott Momaday gave a whole variety of them: he used Pueblo, Kiowa and Navajo mythology, and even a Christian story in Tosamah's sermon – "The Gospel According to John".[143] In *Ceremony* original names of deities and heroes are usually used with their dubbing in English ("Ts'its'tsi'nako, Thought-Woman", "Iktoa'ak'o'ya – Reed Woman", "Ma'see'wi and Ou'yu'ye'wi the twin brothers", etc.). This immerses the reader in the atmosphere of Native American traditions and customs. In *House Made of Dawn* mostly English versions of the names are used ("Turquoise Woman's son", "the Bear Maiden", etc.), but in the last story an American Indian name is also introduced: "*Esdzá shash nadle*, or *Dzil quigi*". Not giving original names may serve the purpose of stating how close an

---

[143] Momaday, N.S. House Made of Dawn. N.Y.: Signet, 1969. P. 84.

American Indian's and a white man's worlds are, how interrelated they are, especially bearing in mind Momaday's bicultural interests. American Indian words are met in both novels, but most of all in *House Made of Dawn*, which starts ("*Dypaloh*") and finishes ("*Qtsedaba*") with them[144].

Also, words that have already become part of English vocabulary are often met – kiva, hogan, peyote and others, which make the necessary settings and create the American Indian atmosphere in the novels. In both books traditional ceremonies and rituals are described: hunting rites (deer hunting in *Ceremony* – pp. 53-54; bear hunting in *House Made of Dawn* – pp. 178-184), burial ceremonies (*House Made of Dawn*, pp. 57, 189), also a typical peyote ceremony (*House Made of Dawn*, pp. 101-106), and traditional feasts and dances (e.g., the Feast of Santiago in *House Made of Dawn*), as well as the mythological patterns of healing. All this gives a wonderful perspective of cultural and spiritual life of Native Americans (in our case — of the South-West).

---

[144] Dypaloh — "the opening formula for storytelling in Jemez (the phrase "Once upon a time" is such a formula in English). When the audience hears this word, they know that what follows will be a story." Qtsedaba — "this closing formula signals the end of a story (Jemez)." (Study Help Full Glossary / House Made of Dawn, [online] Available at: https://www.cliffsnotes.com/literature/h/house-made-of-dawn/study-help/full-glossary [Accessed 30 June 2017].)

4.6. The Role of Stories, Songs and the Word for American Indians

We have already discussed the role of the word in the life of American Indians and the way it is perceived by them; now we would like to look at how this topic is reflected in the novels.

The best concept of the word is found in Tosamah's, the Priest of the Sun's, sermon in *House Made of Dawn*, where he starts with Saint John's words "In the beginning was the Word..." and goes on analyzing the word in the white culture and at the same time compared such attitude with his grandmother's and thus of all American Indians. All his sermon underlines the importance of the word as a creative power:

> It was dark, and there was nothing. ... there was darkness all around, and in the darkness something happened. ... It was almost nothing in itself, a single sound, a word – a word broken off at the darkest center of the night and let go in the awful void, forever and forever. And it was almost nothing in itself. It scarcely was; but it *was*, and everything began.[145]

Then Tosamah describes how, in his opinion, Saint John wrote the Gospel: he had a

---

[145] Momaday, N.S. House Made of Dawn. N.Y.: Signet, 1969. P. 85.

revelation about the Word, it was only an instant, some vision, and he wondered what it was. It was the Truth. And here, instead of simply saying so, "he went on because he was a preacher. The perfect vision faded from his mind, and he went on. ... He made a complex sentence of the Truth, two sentences, three, a paragraph. He made a sermon and theology of the Truth"[146], and that was his mistake. "He could find no satisfaction in the simple fact that the Word *was*..."[147] At this moment Tosamah starts to compare the whites and American Indians, and the main difference is that for a white man the Word is just a common instrument, while for an American Indian it is magic:

> ... the white man has his ways. ... He talks about the Word. He talks through it and around it. He builds upon it with syllables, with prefixes and suffixes, and hyphens and accents. He adds and divides and multiplies the Word. And in all of this he subtracts the Truth.[148]

"The white man takes such things as words and literatures for granted, as indeed he must, for nothing in his world is so commonplace. On every

---

[146] Momaday, N.S. House Made of Dawn. N.Y.: Signet, 1969. P. 87.
[147] Ibid., p. 90.
[148] Ibid., p. 87.

side of him there are words by the millions..."[149] And right here, as an opposition, goes the explanation of what the Word means for Native Americans (on the example of the Priest of the Sun's grandmother) – something "sacred and eternal", "a timeless, *timeless* thing"[150], "the almighty Word"[151]: "She had learned that in words and in language, and there only, she could have whole and consummate being."[152] Thus, the perception of the universe is completely different, from the very beginning – from the moment of creation, from the very first word, and it is projected to all life. For Tosamah's grandmother, like for any American Indian, "words were medicine[153]; they were magic and invisible. They came from nothing into sound and meaning. They were beyond price; they could neither be bought nor sold. And she never threw words away."[154] But for the white man the "regard for language – for the Word itself – as an instrument of creation has diminished nearly to the point of no return. It may be that he will perish by the Word."[155]

---

[149] Momaday, N.S. House Made of Dawn. N.Y.: Signet, 1969. P. 89.
[150] Ibid., p. 88.
[151] Ibid., p. 86.
[152] Ibid., p. 88.
[153] For the explanation of "medicine", see Part 1.3.
[154] Momaday, N.S. House Made of Dawn. N.Y.: Signet, 1969. P. 89.
[155] Ibid.

From the understanding of the meaning of the word goes American Indians' attitude to stories and songs. The role of stories has also been outlined above, and here we would only like to precise it a little more and to add some points found in the novels under study. As already said, Native Americans know the value of the word and do not use it in vain (paraphrasing the second Commandment, theirs might sound like "Thou shalt not use the Word in vain"); "silence was the older and better part of custom."[156] That is why if they tell stories those are full of meaning and wisdom. "Storytelling; to utter and to hear...' And the simple act of listening is crucial to the concept of language, and more crucial even than reading and writing, and language in turn is crucial to human society."[157] American Indian stories are told "carefully, slowly and at length, because they [are] ... old and true, and they ... [can] be lost forever."[158] Words can cure, like the songs of medicine men or the Night Chant of Benally ("I used to tell him about those old ways, the stories and the things, Beautyway and Night Chant. I sang some of those things, and I told him what they meant, what I thought they were about"[159]).

---

[156] Ibid., p. 57.
[157] Ibid., p. 88.
[158] Ibid., p. 178.

"The stories are intended to *do* something at least as much as they are intended to *say* something".[160] Songs are very difficult to be separated from stories as they also tell things, but mainly these are some impressions and feelings, like the song about a horse in *House Made of Dawn*, or prayers, like "House Made of Dawn" or the one people had for the sunrise in *Ceremony*. All stories are usually told by the elders of the tribe, because elders are greatly respected and their experience is much greater than the others', that is why young American Indians often remember listening to their grandparents' stories in childhood:

> *And that night your grandfather hammered the strips of silver and told you stories in the firelight. And you were little and right there in the center of everything, the sacred mountains, the snow-covered mountains and the hills, the gullies and the flats, the sundowns and the night, everything – where you were little, where you were and had to be.*[161]

---

[159] Momaday, N.S. House Made of Dawn. N.Y.: Signet, 1969. P. 133.

[160] Gill, S.D., Sullivan, I.F. Dictionary of Native American Mythology. NY – Oxford: Oxford University Press, 1992. P. XII.

[161] Momaday, N.S. House Made of Dawn. N.Y.: Signet, 1969. P. 143.

For an American Indian the whole world is made of sacred words and holy stories, and he pays them due respect, because they are perceived as true and speak about things that surround us, live things:

> Everywhere he looked, he saw a world made of stories, the long ago, time immemorial stories, as old Grandma called them. It was a world alive, always changing and moving; and if you knew where to look, you could see it, sometimes almost imperceptible, like the motion of the stars across the sky.[162]

Sometimes a song can express everything, even what cannot be expressed in mere words, and can embrace the whole soul of a person, like at the end of the novel a song leads Abel back to his tribe and traditions: "He was running, and under his breath he began to sing. There was no sound, and he had no voice; he had only the words of a song. And he went running on the rise of the song. *House made of pollen, house made of dawn.*"[163] Not without reason their songs are called "chants" – repeated words, often used for religious prayers. "An American Indian is born with the almighty Word, stories and songs composed of it, lives with them, and dies with

---

[162] Ibid., p. 100.
[163] Ibid., p. 191.

them"[164], like Abel's grandfather: "He revived in the dawn, and he knew who Abel was, and he talked and sang"[165] for six mornings till he died on the seventh...

---

[164] Данчевская, О.Е. Американские индейцы в этнокультурной политике США конца 20 – начала 21 вв. М.: Прометей МПГУ, 2009. С. 103.
[165] Momaday, N.S. House Made of Dawn. N.Y.: Signet, 1969. P. 175.

CONCLUSION

Some general acquaintance with Native American mythology, history and worldview, as well as the analysis of the novels *Ceremony* by Leslie Marmon Silko and *House Made of Dawn* by N. Scott Momaday, have helped us to come to several conclusions, the most important of which, in our opinion, are the following:

1) Myth and mythology have a variety of forms in which they are manifested, but these forms differ from culture to culture. In Native American cultures they can be presented in (holy) stories and songs/chants, as well as performed during ceremonies. There are many specific features in tribal mythologies, but there are also a great number of general ones, which proves that the tribes, though not always friendly with each other, are united by some superiour destination. Pueblo mythology makes part of Native American one, but it has its own set of deities and myths (often paralleling the general thread).

2) Mythology plays a crucial role in American Indian life. In spite of the fact that at the present time publishing has almost replaced storytelling, the latter

together with the songs and chants performed during ancient rituals still remains vital in the life of every tribe.

3) Originally Native American literature (mainly mythology) was presented in an oral form, but it has changed greatly since the beginning of the previous century – it has proclaimed its place in written form as well. More than that, Native American writers have occupied a prominent and a very stable place in the world literature.

4) The history of American Indians was full of difficulties, outward intrusions and influences, but despite all, those peoples have preserved their culture. They showed extreme strength of character manifested in stubborn resistance to the whites – meeting sufferings and sorrows, they fought for their rights. Even now far from all the problems are solved.

5) The study of the two novels for the use of Native American mythology in them has proven that in *House Made of Dawn* and *Ceremony* the writers managed to bring the American Indian world to the reader, introduce Native American traditions to him, efficiently and skilfully use stories and songs for different

stylistic purposes, the main of which was to introduce the Native American world outlook to the reader.

6) The attitude to the word presented in the novels characterises perfectly well the American Indian soul: for Native Americans, the word in a sacred thing, which differs greatly from the attitude of the whites to it and to mythology. Both novels "emphasize the creative power of the word"[166], which is most important to understand and to accept for anyone.

Native American authors give the reader an opportunity to comprehend sometimes a strange for him, but such a beautiful world of American Indians, their mythology and culture through original works of prose and poetry which are now available to the wide audience.

The works of Native Americans are not just literary heritage, but centuries-old wisdom, collected on the pages of novels, stories, poems by the authors living in the world of Euro-Americans and aware of all its problems, but at the same time not losing touch with their traditions and

---

[166] Bedeaux, M.D. Astronomical Patterns in Novels of Frank Waters, N. Scott Momaday, and Leslie Marmon Silko, [online] Available at:
<http://www.unm.edu/~abqteach/ArcheoCUs/99-01-01.pdf> [Accessed 10 January 2002].

mythology. Such books help to better understand the culture of American Indians, and, as a result, understand them themselves, which is essential in the modern multicultural society, because "not a person's worldview realizes itself through texts, images and rituals, but rather an accessible (inherited from past generations or borrowed) set of texts, images and scenarios of rituals form a world outlook."[167]

That is, works of ethnic literature open for the reader the magical world of mythology and culture, as well as ample opportunities for self-knowledge and self-improvement. It has long been proven that there are archetypal (mythological) models in each of us, in general they are the same throughout the world, and they are realized in our perception of reality and behavior. And this means that one needs to know them. As J. Campbell believed, "The effective mythology, which originated in the crypts of the psyche, returns the person to the soul (the "center of the circle") — and anyone who will follows its

---

[167] Березкин, Ю.Е. Мифология аборигенов Америки: результаты статистической обработки ареального распределения мотивов // История и семиотика индейских культур Америки. Под ред. А.А. Бородатовой, В.А. Тишкова. М.: Наука, 2002. С. 277-346. С. 278.

guiding signs with sufficient seriousness, will rediscover them in himself"[168].[169]

---

[168] Кэмпбелл, Дж. Мифы, в которых нам жить. Киев: София, 2002. С. 244.

[169] Данчевская, О.Е. Мифы североамериканских индейцев в романах «Церемония» Л.М. Силко и «Дом, из рассвета сотворенный» Н.Скотта Момадэя // Актуальные проблемы исследования англоязычных литератур: международный сборник научых статей. Классики и современники. Минск: РИВШ, 2008. Вып. 7. С. 174-183. С. 182-3.

BIBLIOGRAPHY

alt.mythology General FAQ ver. 1.8, [online] Available at: <http://members.bellatlantic.net/~vze33gpz/mythgenfaq.html#A2A> [Accessed 05 April 2002].

Austgen, S.M. Leslie Marmon Silko's Ceremony and the Effect of White Contact on Pueblo Myth and Ritual, [online] Available at: <http://history.hanover.edu/hhr/hhr93_2.html> [Accessed 14 January 2007].

Bedeaux, M.D. Astronomical Patterns in Novels of Frank Waters, N. Scott Momaday, and Leslie Marmon Silko, [online] Available at: <http://www.unm.edu/~abqteach/ArcheoCUs/99-01-01.pdf> [Accessed 10 January 2002].

Bordewich, F.M. Killing the White Man's Indian: Reinventing Native Americans at the End of the Twentieth Century. NY: Anchor Books, 1997.

Cirlot, J.E. A Dictionary of Symbols. London: Routledge, 1971.

Danchevskaya, O.Y. Concept of Soul among North American Indians. Where No One Else Has Gone Before: Proceedings of the Ninth Native American Symposium. Durant, Oklahoma: Southeastern Oklahoma State University, 2012. P. 89-96. (Also available online at: <http://homepages.se.edu/nas/files/2013/03/NAS-2011-Proceedings-Danchevskaya.pdf>)

Danchevskaya, O.Y. Stereotyping American Indians. Sixty-Seven Nations and Counting: *Proceedings of the Seventh Native American Symposium*. Ed. by Mark B. Spencer and Rachel Tudor. Durant, Oklahoma: Southeastern Oklahoma State University, 2008. P.112-117. (Also available online at:

<http://homepages.se.edu/nas/files/2013/03/NAS-2007-Proceedings-Danchevskaya.pdf>)

Danchevskaya, O.Y. Numbers in American Indian Mythology. Native Leadership: Past, Present and Future. Proceedings of the Eleventh Native American Symposium. Durant, Oklahoma: Southeastern Oklahoma State University, 2017. - in press

Danchevskaya, O.Y. Turquoise in the Life of American Indians. Images, Imaginations, and Beyond. *Proceedings of the Eighth Native American Symposium*. Ed. by Mark B. Spencer. Durant, Oklahoma: Southeastern Oklahoma State University, 2010. P. 144-149. P. 146. (Also available online at: <http://homepages.se.edu/nas/files/2013/03/NAS-2009-Proceedings-Danchevskaya.pdf>)

Gill, S.D., Sullivan, I.F. Dictionary of Native American Mythology. NY – Oxford: Oxford University Press, 1992.

Heyrman, Ch.L. Native American Religion in Early America, [online] Available at: <http://www.nhc.rtp.nc.us:8080/tserve/eighteen/ekeyinfo/natrel.htm> [Accessed 30 November 2001].

Information in this chapter is partially taken from: Native American, [online] Available at: <http://www.bright.net/~jimsjems/native.html> [Accessed 10 February 2002].

Momaday, N.S. House Made of Dawn. NY: Signet, 1969.

Moore, M. Genocide of the Mind: New Native American Writing. NY: Thunder's Mouth Press/Nation Books, 2003.

Native American Mythology, [online] Available at: <http://portalproductions.com/h/native_american.htm> [Accessed 24 February 2002].

Nelson, R.M. Place and Vision. The Function of Landscape in Native American Fiction. 1999, [online] Available at:

<http://www.richmond.edu/~rnelson/PandV/front.html> [Accessed 25 December 2001].

Prucha, F.P. American Indian Treaties: The History of a Political Anomaly. Berkeley etc.: Univ. of California Press, 1997.

Prucha, F.P. The Indians in American Society: From the Revolutionary War to the Present. Berkeley etc.: Univ. of California Press, 1985.

Radin, P. The Basic Myth of North American Indians // Eranos-Jahrbuch: Der Mensch und die Mythische Welt, Band XVII (1949). Zurich: Rhein-Verlag, 1950. P. 359-419.

Radin, P. The Trickster. A Study in Native American Mythology. N.Y.: Philosophical Library, 1956.

Robinson, B.A. Native American Spirituality, [online] Available at: <http://www.religioustolerance.org/nataspir.htm> [Accessed 13 February 2002].

Ryan, J.B. Listening to Native Americans // Listening: Journal of Religion and Culture, Vol. 31, No.1 Winter 1996 pp. 24-36, [online] Available at: <http://www.op.org/DomCentral/library/native.htm> [Accessed 06 March 2002].

Silko, L.M. Ceremony. NY: Signet, 1978.

Study Help Full Glossary / House Made of Dawn, [online] Available at: https://www.cliffsnotes.com/literature/h/house-made-of-dawn/study-help/full-glossary [Accessed 30 June 2017].
The Role of Storytelling in Native American Cultures, [online] Available at: <http://homepages.uni-tuebingen.de/student/afra.korfmann/story.htm> [Accessed 21 March 2002].
Webster Dictionary, [online] Available at: <http://www.webster.com> [Accessed 25 March 2002].

Бауэр, В., Дюмоц, И., Головин, С. Энциклопедия символов. Москва: КРОН-ПРЕСС, 1995. С. 84.

Березкин, Ю.Е. Мифология аборигенов Америки: результаты статистической обработки ареального распределения мотивов // История и семиотика индейских культур Америки. Под ред. А.А. Бородатовой, В.А. Тишкова. Москва: Наука, 2002. С. 277-346.

Бирлайн, Дж.Ф. Параллельная мифология. Москва: КРОН-ПРЕСС, 1997.

Ващенко, А.В. Суд Париса. Сравнительная мифология в культуре и цивилизации. Москва: ФИЯиР МГУ, 2008.

Ващенко, А.В. Культура, мифология и фольклор американских индейцев доколониальной эпохи. // История литературы США. Т.1. Москва: Наследие, 1997. С. 39-88.

Ващенко, А.В. Столб, подпирающий мир: традиция и современность на Хайда Гвай. Владения гитксанов. Ногинск: АНАЛИТИКА РОДИС, 2012.

Данчевская, О.Е. Американские индейцы в этнокультурной политике США конца 20 – начала 21 вв. Москва: Прометей МПГУ, 2009.

Данчевская, О.Е. Индейское наследие в американской культуре // Сборник материалов Международной конференции «Язык, культура, речевое общение»: К 85-летию профессора Марка Яковлевича Блоха. В двух частях. Москва: Прометей, 2009. Часть 1. С. 170-173.

Данчевская, О.Е. Исторические предания, легенды и мифы севеоамериканских индейцев как дополнительный этнологический источник // Источники и историография по антропологии народов Америки. Москва: ИЭА РАН, 2017. С. 261-274.

Данчевская, О.Е. Мифы североамериканских индейцев в романах «Церемония» Л.М. Силко и «Дом, из рассвета сотворенный» Н.Скотта Момадэя // Актуальные проблемы исследования англоязычных литератур: международный сборник научых статей. Классики и современники. Минск: РИВШ, 2008. Вып. 7. С. 174-183.

Данчевская, О.Е. Сверхъестественная власть и её носители в мифах о Первотворении индейцев Юго-Запада США // Антропология власти: Феномен власти в аборигенной Америке. Москва: Наука, 2006. С. 428-438.

Данчевская, О.Е. Слово как источник силы. Устные традиции в современной жизни североамериканских индейцев // Материалы 31 и 32 международных конференций ОИКС «Слово и/как власть: авторство и авторитет в американской культурной традиции» и «Америка реальная, воображаемая и виртуальная». – Москва: Фак-т журналистики МГУ им. Ломоносова, 2006. С. 59-66.

Данчевская, О.Е. Солнце в мифологии и жизни индейцев Северной Америки // Феномен творческой личности в культуре. Материалы VI международной конференции. Москва: МГУ, 2014. С. 36-46.

Данчевская, О.Е. Цветовая символика в культурах североамериканских индейцев // Город и урбанизм в американской культуре. Материалы XXXVII международной конференции Российского общества по изучению культуры США. Москва: Фак-т журналистики МГУ, 2014. С. 264-280.

Кремо, М.А. Деволюция человека: Ведическая альтернатива теории Дарвина, [online] Available at: <http://bookz.ru/authors/maikl-kremo/devoluci_690/1-devoluci_690.html> [Accessed September 20 2015].

Кэмпбелл, Дж. Мифы, в которых нам жить. Киев: София, 2002.

Леви-Строс, К. Путь масок. Москва: Республика, 2000.

Мелетинский, Е.М. (ред.) Мифологический словарь. Москва: Советская энциклопедия, 1991.

Олкотт, У.Т. Мифы о солнце. Москва: ЗАО Центрполиграф, 2013.

Токарев, С.А. (ред.). Мифы народов мира: Энциклопедия в 2 т. Москва: Советская Энциклопедия, 1991.

Тэйлор, Э. Первобытная культура: В 2 кн. Москва: ТЕРРА – Книжный клуб, 2009.

Элиаде, М. Шаманизм. Киев: София, 1998.

CPSIA information can be obtained
at www.ICGtesting.com
Printed in the USA
LVHW082152070322
712875LV00027B/824